THE
GREEN
CLEANSE
BIBLE

THE
GREEN
CLEANSE
BIBLE

Programs and recipes to lose weight,
boost energy, and flush toxins

Karen Inge
Luisa Adam

THUNDER BAY
P · R · E · S · S
SAN DIEGO

Thunder Bay Press
An imprint of Printers Row Publishing Group
10350 Barnes Canyon Road, Suite 100, San Diego CA 92121
www.thunderbaybooks.com

Moseley Road Inc., www.moseleyroad.com
Publisher: Sean Moore
Authors: Karen Inge and Luisa Adam
Consultant Dietitian: Danielle Bowman
Interior layout and design: Emma Borghesi
Cover design: OilOften Graphic Design, www.oiloften.co.uk

Thunder Bay Press
Publisher: Peter Norton
Publishing Team: Lori Asbury, Ana Parker, Laura Vignale
Editorial Team: JoAnn Padgett, Melinda Allman, J. Carroll, Traci Douglas
Production Team: Blake Mitchum, Rusty von Dyl

Library of Congress Cataloging-in-Publication Data:
Inge, Karen.
    The green cleanse Bible / Karen Inge and Luisa Adam.
        pages cm
    ISBN 978-1-62686-435-1 (hardcover)
1. Smoothies (Beverages) 2. Vegetable juices. 3. Detoxification (Health) 4.
Nutrition. I. Adam, Luisa. II. Title.
    TX817.S636I54 2015
    641.8'75--dc23
                                        2015005956

Printed in China
19 18 17 16 15   1 2 3 4 5

Disclaimer
The information in this book is of a general nature and is intended to help
you understand issues concerning nutrition and health; it is not a substitute
for professional medical or dietary advice. While all care has been taken in
the preparation of its contents, the Publisher and the Authors accept no
liability for damages arising from information in this book. Please always
consult your doctor or an accredited dietitian for advice specific to your
individual health requirements.

Contents

GREEN SMOOTHIES AREN'T JUST GREEN!

GREEN SMOOTHIES COME IN ALL COLORS AND FLAVORS AND ARE THE EASIEST WAY TO ENSURE THAT YOU AND YOUR FAMILY CONSUME THE RECOMMENDED DAILY ALLOWANCE OF FRUIT AND VEGETABLES—A WHOPPING 4½ CUPS A DAY, WHICH CAN BE DIFFICULT IF YOU CAN'T BRING YOUR CHILD TO FACE A SINGLE CARROT! AND FOR ADULTS, THEY ARE THE QUICK, CONVENIENT, LOW-MESS, AND NUTRITIOUS WAY TO HELP CLEANSE AND ENERGIZE THE BODY, JUMP-START A HEALTH KICK, LOSE A FEW EXTRA POUNDS, HELP WARD OFF HEART DISEASE AND A HOST OF OTHER DISORDERS—AND GENERALLY LOOK AND FEEL TERRIFIC!

SO, LET'S GET STARTED . . .

What Are Green Smoothies?

Green smoothies are highly nutritious blends of fruits and vegetables. Other ingredients such as grains, nuts, seeds, protein powders, and various milks can be added, but the primary ingredients are fruit or vegetables.

There is no doubt that a diet high in plant foods is beneficial to health in numerous ways. Fruits and certain vegetables, as well as grains, provide us with energy in the form of carbohydrates. They also provide an endless number of vitamins and minerals, all of which are minute in size yet play powerful roles in all bodily functions. And diets high in plant foods are inherently high in dietary fiber, and provide some healthy fats and proteins as well. Raw plant foods are widely advocated as part of a balanced diet, because raw fruits and vegetables are generally more nutritious than their cooked counterparts.

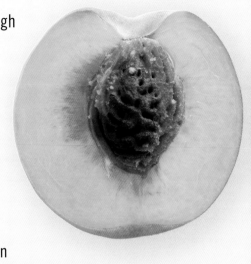

However, it can be difficult to eat enough fruit and vegetables, let alone raw ones. Some people like them but don't have time to eat them. Others, especially children, may dislike the taste, particularly of vegetables. And it is all too easy to eat too many of one type and not enough of another, thereby resulting in shortfalls in certain nutrients. Another problem is that vegetables are often overcooked or smothered in rich, creamy sauces that almost counteract the nutritional gains of eating vegetables in the first place. Seasonal availability can also be a factor, and in this case frozen fruits and vegetables generally offer the same benefits as fresh, and many, such as berries, can take the place of ice blocks in smoothies. Another issue with raw foods is some people find them difficult to eat and somehow less comforting and nurturing than cooked food. These are just some of the reasons that getting enough fruit and vegetables into our daily diets can be a challenge.

At least part of the solution lies in smoothies. They provide a quick and convenient way to blend a wide range of fruits and vegetables into one liquid meal that is highly nutritious. They also minimize waste and mess. They are great for masking the flavor of a less palatable but nutritious ingredient with that of another, delicious food, or for mixing fruits and vegetables with complementary flavors. Flavorful and nutritious herbs and spices can also be added. Furthermore, raw fruits and vegetables are easier to digest when blended into a smoothie. Crunching on hard, fibrous foods such as carrot can be unpleasant or even difficult for some people, but the problem is overcome with blending. It is possible, too, that some raw foods may evoke a negative emotional response in people, because raw fruits and vegetables are largely cold and hard and hence lack the comfort factor of warmer, softer foods. Smooth, luscious smoothies, on the other hand, have a comforting texture.

Smoothies are generally consumed cold, but they can also be used as the basis of raw soups, which can be slightly warmed up to about 110° F without compromising their nutritional value. This is still technically considered "raw." It is important that fresh ingredients are used (or quality frozen ones when necessary), and that the smoothie (or soup) is consumed soon after preparation. If not, smoothies should be refrigerated, which will protect them from significant deterioration for a few hours, but thereafter frozen (perhaps as ice blocks) until ready to use.

Smoothies in Your Diet

Nutritious smoothies may supplement healthy diets or replace one, perhaps occasionally two, meals out of three in a day. An all-liquid diet based on the consumption of smoothies is not recommended and compromises health in other areas. Chewing is very important— as are some nutrients that are difficult to source through fruit and vegetables alone.

One word of caution is that care should be taken with the amounts of ingredients that are added to smoothies. This applies in particular to nuts, seeds, dairy and dairy substitutes, and supplements. Too high a volume of these ingredients can be too high in calories

or pack too much dietary fiber or protein, and hence may have potentially adverse effects on health. Therefore, while the quantities of fruit and vegetables in smoothies can be more or less varied according to personal preference, it is important to keep at least roughly to the amounts of the other ingredients specified in the recipes or, if using purchased supplements such as protein powder, to the amounts specified on their packaging. In the case of these additional ingredients, more is not necessarily better. And, although fruit smoothies are particularly delicious because of their sweetness, try to bulk them up with at least some less calorie-dense vegetables. They'll still be sweet—the flavor of certain vegetables added to fruit smoothies will be imperceptible—but they'll be lower in calories. Fruit is very nutritious, but also high in natural sugars, so fruit-and-vegetable smoothies make for a healthier combination.

In certain circumstances, short bouts of all-liquid diets might be appropriate for specific medical reasons, or perhaps to make up the two-day low-calorie component of a 5:2 fast diet (see p. 237), or even just to give the body a rest. But, for the most part, healthy smoothies should be just one part—even if a rather large part— of an overall healthy diet.

Anybody with pre-existing medical conditions should of course consult with a doctor or health practitioner before making any sudden changes to their diet.

About This Book

The book includes 100 smoothie recipes that should be used as a launching pad into your own personal smoothie adventure. It is intended to inspire and to show how well certain ingredients combine together in a smoothie, both in terms of flavor and nutrition. It also details eight eating plans that support healthy lifestyles. These plans map back to some of the smoothie recipes and provide several food recipes that complement the smoothies.

Also included is a broad introduction to the vast and complex field of nutrition; information about various fruits, vegetables, and other common smoothie ingredients, including supplements; some background on equipment; our top 10 tips for making smoothies; and finally an index, a list of references, and acknowledgments.

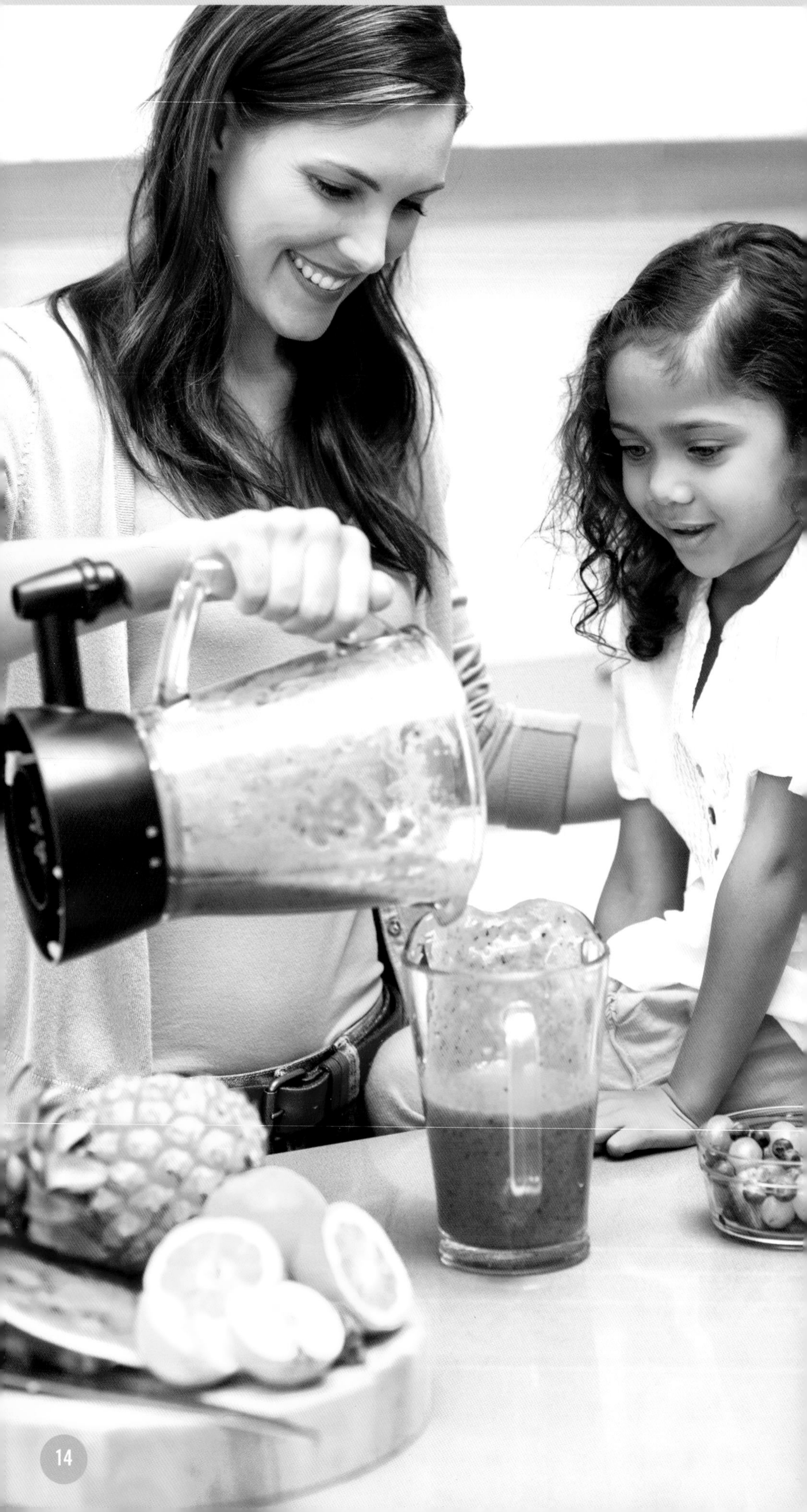

EQUIPMENT

Not much equipment is needed for making smoothies. The whole point is that they are quick, easy to make, not complicated, not messy—but wonderfully nutritious. Really, the only major piece of equipment for making smoothies is a good-quality blender.

You may or may not need a glass from which to drink the smoothie—in some of the powerful modern blenders, the mixing vessel is also the drinking receptacle, making them super quick and easy to use and to clean up afterward.

You'll also need at least one good knife, together with a chopping board, to roughly peel or cut up the ingredients as needed. Other items that are useful but not essential include scales and measuring cups (if you are particular about the weights and volumes of certain ingredients, perhaps for calorie-counting purposes), peelers, graters (helpful if you want to garnish the smoothie with a sprinkle of lemon zest, or for grating small amounts of whole nutmeg or ginger into the blend), everyday spoons and spatulas to help with serving—and perhaps a wooden spoon for bashing the seeds out of pomegranates. But all these things are found in most kitchens. Let's move on!

Blenders

When it comes to using blenders for making smoothies, there are three main types: the jug-style blenders long used for blending milkshakes, smoothies, and other concoctions; the new breed of powerful "nutrient-extracting" upside-down blenders, such as the Nutri Ninja™ and NutriBullet™; and finally the humble handheld blender. If you are using one of the first two types mentioned, clear a space on your kitchen counter—close to a power outlet and ideally the fruit bowl—and keep it there, ready for use whenever a smoothie craving strikes. Don't pack it away where it will fight for space and become increasingly less accessible, so that moments of inspiration disappear in a puff of frustration as you fight to retrieve it from the back of the cupboard.

Know Your Equipment: It is important to know your own blender. Although some general rules apply to all blenders, their capabilities vary—some less powerful blenders, for example, may not be able to crush ice, or must have the ingredients added and blended in steps. Read the manual, be aware of your equipment's particular advantages and limitations, and use it only in accordance with the manufacturer's instructions.

Jug Blenders

The powerful (usually more expensive) types of jug blenders can generally blend most ingredients well, even if they are all loaded into the jug at the same time. Blending times may vary, and will depend on the level of

smoothness desired. Several bursts on high power for 15–30 seconds may be required. Be aware, however, that even some of the more powerful jug blenders do not have the ability to crush ice. If your blender does not handle ice easily, chilled water or slightly softened frozen fruit, such as berries, might be a better option. Ice that has been crushed beforehand can also be used. On the other hand, if you are spending a lot of money on a jug blender, make sure it does crush ice! Powerful blenders are a great choice—not only can they handle tough ingredients, but their ability to finely grind ingredients most likely enables more nutrients to be released. Don't, however, be tempted to load indiscriminate amounts of nuts, seeds, supplements, and other non-produce ingredients into the blender just because you can; overloading with some ingredients can have adverse health effects, while pulverizing others can release toxins that cannot be digested.

Making the Smoothie: When using a jug-style blender, especially a less powerful one, place ice in the bottom of the jug, followed by the liquid. Add supplements, nuts, seeds, and grains at this point if you are using them, then the soft ingredients, such as spinach, herbs, and soft fruits. Load the heavier ingredients, such as apples and pears, last. Top up with extra fluid if needed. If you have a very powerful blender, mix everything together in one go. If your blender is less powerful, you may need to blend in steps, first blending the ice, liquid, and leafy vegetables, before progressing through the rest.

Ninjas™, NutriBullets™, and Other "Nutrient-Extracting" Blenders

These are the super-powerful upside-down blenders that use a large bottle-like vessel or beaker instead of a jug to hold the ingredients (the "vessel"). The vessel is filled with the ingredients before being screwed into a lid that also holds (very securely) the powerful blades. It is then inserted upside-down (with lid and blades at the bottom) into the machine. The beauty of this design is twofold: First, when blending is complete, the vessel is removed from the machine and the lid is taken off; the smoothie can then either be drunk straight from the vessel or tipped into other glasses. Second, cleanup is a breeze. The lid is quick and easy to wash, and because the vessel is also used as a drinking cup, there are fewer utensils to wash. There are also claims that the most powerful of these types of blenders are able to extract additional nutrients from fruit and vegetables.

These machines also come with extra lids (without blades!) that are used to seal the smoothies inside the vessel if they are not consumed right away. This makes it portable, preventing spills and keeping particles in the air from entering, and also suitable for short-term storage in the fridge. Most also have drinking spouts—a practical and fun design that is popular with kids and teenagers.

Making the Smoothie: In this type of blender, the ingredients are put into the vessel in the opposite order as in jug blenders, and then it is inverted. First, in go the fruit and vegetables, followed by any nuts, seeds, and supplements, then the liquids, and finally the ice. Then it is just a matter of screwing on the lid, inserting the vessel upside-down into the machine, and blending the ingredients.

Handheld Blenders

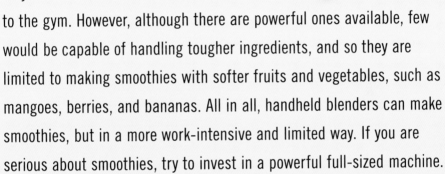

Handheld blenders can be quite useful and have the advantage of being portable, so they can be taken on vacation, to work, and to the gym. However, although there are powerful ones available, few would be capable of handling tougher ingredients, and so they are limited to making smoothies with softer fruits and vegetables, such as mangoes, berries, and bananas. All in all, handheld blenders can make smoothies, but in a more work-intensive and limited way. If you are serious about smoothies, try to invest in a powerful full-sized machine.

Making the Smoothie: Most likely, you will need to cube the fruits and vegetables before blending. Start by putting small amounts of diced ingredients and liquid into a suitable vessel, then begin blending. Add more ingredients and liquid as you go, blending them all together between additions. Some experimentation might be needed.

NUTRIENTS AND NUTRITION

Nutrition, Cleansing, and Detoxing

The terms "cleansing" and "detoxing" mean different things to different people. It may refer to your body's own ability, when it is properly nourished, to efficiently rid itself of the substances it does not need and utilize the substances it does need. There is no one diet or food that can promise a body that functions at its optimum, and the issue is further complicated by the fact that what may be "toxic" to one person may be highly beneficial to another. Furthermore, some essential nutrients are paradoxically toxic if consumed in high quantities.

Perhaps the best definition of "cleansing" and "detoxing" programs is that they are nutritionally balanced programs focused on simplified eating habits and fresh, unprocessed foods. They therefore support the body's own cleansing system in the most effective way. It might also be true that such programs may be less likely to introduce so-called "toxins" into the body in the first place. Smoothies made from fresh fruit and vegetables, perhaps with some grains and milk or yogurt added, are an extremely effective and simple way of increasing your intake of nutrients.

Nutrients found in food enable the systems and organs of the body to function in their intended ways. These include the digestive tract, kidneys, lungs, skin, liver, lymphatic system, and respiratory system, which are each directly involved in the body's own detoxification processes. They cleanse the body by breaking down compounds into other forms that are then excreted through waste (urine and fecal matter), sweat, and breathing. Certain nutrients also promote the health of the cardiovascular system in various ways. For example, some help to keep arteries clean and flexible by preventing plaque from building up in them.

Vitamins, minerals, and phytonutrients are vitally important to the body's own cleansing processes. These are the minute substances found in food that enable chemical processes to occur within the body's systems and organs (see pages 25–35). Many of these substances support the immune system, protect cells, reduce or prevent inflammation, and help fight infection. Some are even thought to help ward off certain cancers. Others facilitate the release of energy, which is one of many reasons why eating fresh, unprocessed, natural foods does help boost energy levels. Some are needed for the effective metabolism of fats and carbohydrates, and for the building of healthy cells. Yet others facilitate the production of hormones and enable their myriad of functions in the body, including some directly related to its detoxification. The list is endless, the processes complex, and yet the easiest way to support the body's own cleansing system is through good nutrition.

What Are Nutrients?

Nutrients are the substances found in food that support and enable life. They enter the body through food and are not made by the body itself. Once absorbed into the body, they work alone or in combination with other substances to facilitate all the chemical interactions and bodily functions that occur within. Without nutrients, we could not grow, think, or otherwise exist. They are essential for the functioning of the human body and for its maintenance and repair.

There seems to be an infinite number of nutrients in food, including the fat-soluble vitamins A, D, E, and K as well as the water-soluble vitamins B complex and C; minerals such as calcium, magnesium, iron, and zinc; fats such as omega-3; proteins such as the amino acids found in legumes, meat, and dairy products; and carbohydrates, including the sugars found in fruit. Fiber and water are also considered nutrients.

Nutrients are found in all foods, including meat, grains, fats, and produce. Of course, overconsumption of certain nutrients such as saturated fats, sugars, and sodium (salt) is not beneficial for our health. Some foods, like sugary drinks and chips, have a low nutrient density, which means that even though they are a source of calories (energy), they provide little or no nutritional value. If you want to have a healthy diet, then it is important to eat foods that have a high nutrient density—lots of nutrients for the calories. Fresh fruits and vegetables are good examples of foods that have a high nutrient density.

Essential Nutrients

There are seven categories of nutrients that are known as "essential" because they are necessary for health, growth, and life itself. Without them, we would not exist. They are:

- Vitamins
- Minerals
- Carbohydrates
- Proteins
- Fats (including oils)
- Fiber
- Water

Vitamins and minerals are known as "micronutrients" because only minute quantities are needed to enable the proper functioning of the body. Carbohydrates, proteins, and fats are known as "macronutrients," and are needed in larger quantities. Individual foods contain both macronutrients and micronutrients. For example, carrots are a good source of the macronutrient carbohydrate and also of vitamin A, a micronutrient. Fiber may also be classified as a

macronutrient, as it is needed in large amounts for the body to function properly. Life-giving water is in a class of its own because it is found in every cell in the body, is essential for the transportation of fluids within the body, and enables chemical reactions to occur, among a whole range of other functions.

What About Phytochemicals?

Importantly, there is an emergent group of micronutrients that is variously referred to as "phytonutrients," "phytochemicals," and "phytofoods." This book calls them phytonutrients or phytochemicals. Phytochemicals are naturally occurring substances found in plants. They appear to be extremely beneficial to health but are in the early stages of scientific validation and have not, as yet, been classified as essential nutrients. Nonetheless, indications are that this is a promising area of research that is likely to have huge implications in preventative health practices (as people make lifestyle and dietary changes), as well as in treatments and remedies, and may eventually revolutionize our understanding of the health benefits of fresh fruit and vegetables.

Many phytonutrients have antioxidant properties, meaning they minimize damage caused to the body by harmful molecules called free radicals. Phytonutrients include beta-carotene (one of many carotenoids, which are the plant pigments that give carrots and other red-orange-yellow produce their color), anthocyanins (the blue pigment that colors berries and beets), chlorophyll (the green pigment found in green fruits and vegetables), and the catechins found in black and green tea. Other phytonutrients are phytates (found in beans, brans, and whole grains), curcumins (found in turmeric and mustard), lignans (found in plant seeds such as flaxseed and certain produce), allicin (found in garlic and onion), and ellagic acid (found in grapes, strawberries, apples, and other fruit). A good rule of thumb is to eat a wide range of colored fruits and vegetables—sometimes described as a "food rainbow"—because the yellows, purples, and greens are indicative of the phytochemicals within.

The tables on pages 30–35 summarize many of the known (scientifically proven) roles that many important vitamins and minerals play in our diet, together with their sources and benefits. The tables are not comprehensive, as the scope of the subject is so vast, but they include what nutrients are, to date, generally considered the most important. Where relevant, the tables also allude to emerging knowledge, which is often rooted in folk medicine. The tables differentiate between proven and folk knowledge, the latter of which has not been verified scientifically.

Vitamins and Minerals

Vitamins and minerals are chemical substances found in food. They support and maintain health and enable chemical processes to occur, including the conversion of carbohydrates into energy and the production of hormones by the body's glands. In some cases, they have a preventative role, helping to protect the body from disease.

Folk Medicine and Practice: The phrase "not scientifically proven" can sometimes undermine the validity of certain established folk practices that on face value may seem effective, even we do not yet know why. It does not always mean "proven to be false." Experience has shown that it pays to respect the centuries-old knowledge we have acquired about fresh food and its role in promoting health. Many folk practices have, over time, been proven to have a scientific basis, and so have shed their "folk" status and taken their place among the canons of proven knowledge. Others are the subject of continuing research, or are yet to be investigated. Some caution is needed here, however. Grouped with seemingly well-established folk practices are others that may be entirely false, are scams, are detrimental to health, or have been proven to be false. This is a highly contentious area, but common sense suggests we should pay greatest heed to claims that have been scientifically proven, observe how we respond both physically and mentally to certain foods, and disregard anything that is potentially dangerous, seems too extreme, or is otherwise unfounded.

A varied and nutritious diet should, for the most part, provide all the vitamins and minerals that our bodies need. In certain situations, manufactured vitamin and mineral supplements are useful—for example, in cases of severe deficiency, or when higher doses are required for the treatment of certain conditions, or if people are following very restricted diets, or if locally available foods are deficient in specific nutrients; however, as the name itself implies, supplements should indeed be used only to supplement rather than replace the vitamins and minerals sourced through fresh food.

Another important consideration is that the range of nutrients available through manufactured supplements is limited by the extent of our knowledge. While there is a wealth of both scientifically proven and folk knowledge about specific vitamins and minerals, it is nonetheless still evolving—with no signs of an ending yet in sight. Continuing research is constantly revealing the myriad of ways that vitamins and minerals interact with our bodies, both on their own and in combination with other nutrients and substances in the body.

Vitamins and minerals are, of course, also found in other foods, but fresh produce offers a great variety, together with other valuable components such as phytonutrients, fatty acids, and all-important fiber. Fruit and vegetables are also relatively cheap, readily available, delicious, and easy to prepare. Enough said!

Vitamins are needed in minute quantities in the body to ensure its proper functioning. They are classified into two groups: "water soluble" and "fat soluble".

The fat-soluble vitamins—A, D, E, and K—are stored in the body. This means they are less susceptible to deficiencies than water-soluble vitamins, but at the same time excesses building up in the body over time can result in unpleasant side effects.

Water-soluble vitamins—B-group and C—dissolve in the body's fluids, and excesses are excreted in urine. Because water-soluble vitamins are not stored in the body, they must be replenished frequently. The following tables outline some important vitamins.

Vitamin A

This fat-soluble vitamin is found in plant foods in the form of carotenoids, the pigments that give carrots and other red–orange–yellow plant foods their distinctive colors. The body converts some of the carotenoids into vitamin A. Carotenoids are powerful antioxidants, and of the 500 or more found in nature, the most studied have been beta-carotene, lycopene, zeaxanthin, and beta-cryptoxanthin. Research suggests that these antioxidants may help strengthen the immune system and reduce risk of certain cancers and heart disease.

Vitamin A is needed for:	Good plant sources of vitamin A include
• healthy eyesight, skin, and mucous membranes. • immunity and growth.	bell peppers, carrots, mangoes, cantaloupe, romaine lettuce, sweet potatoes, and dried apricots.

B-Group Vitamins

These water-soluble vitamins are especially important for enabling the body to produce energy, and for keeping the skin, nervous system, and digestive system healthy. They include vitamins B1, B2, B3, B5, B6, B7, B9, and B12, among others. The somewhat confusing omission of some numbers in the naming system is the result of later renaming or reclassification. Some are called by their other names—for example, vitamin B9 is folic acid. Some, such as vitamin B15 (pangamic acid), are not significant enough to include here.

B1 (thiamine):	Good plant sources of vitamin B1 include
• metabolizes carbohydrates and releases energy. • improves appetite and digestion. • supports heart and nervous system.	nuts (macadamia, pistachio, Brazil, pecan, cashew), seeds (sesame, sunflower, chia, pumpkin), green peas, squash, and navy beans.
B2 (riboflavin) helps to: • maintain healthy skin and eyes. • metabolize carbohydrates, protein, and fat, and release energy. • support nervous and digestive systems.	Good plant sources of vitamin B2 include nuts (almond, pistachio, pine, cashew), mushrooms, seeds (sesame, sunflower, pumpkin, chia), spinach, and collard greens.
B3 (niacin): • helps to metabolize carbohydrates, alcohol, and fat, and to release energy in the body. • is essential for growth, and for healthy hair, skin, eyes, liver, and nervous system.	Good plant sources of vitamin B3 include whole grains, nuts, mushrooms, legumes, passion fruit, and avocados.
B5 (pantothenic acid) helps to: • metabolize carbohydrates, protein, fat, and alcohol to release energy. • prevent anemia by assisting in the formation of red blood cells. • produce steroid hormones.	Good plant sources of vitamin B5 include peanuts and legumes.

B6 (pyridoxine) assists in: • protein and carbohydrate metabolism. • formation of red blood cells and prevention of anemia. • production of brain chemicals. • immune function and steroid hormone activity.	Good plant sources of vitamin B6 include whole grains, green leafy vegetables, nuts, and bananas.
B7 (biotin) is needed for: • energy production. • glycogen synthesis.	Good plant sources of vitamin B7 include peanuts, cauliflower, mushrooms, oats, tomatoes, carrots, and walnuts.
B9 (folate) assists in the: • prevention of neural tube defects. • metabolism of DNA. • prevention of anemia. • formation of enzymes and red blood cells. • control of levels of homocysteine, a chemical in the blood that is associated with heart attacks, strokes, and blood clots when it is elevated.	Good plant sources of vitamin B9 include green leafy vegetables, legumes, seeds, whole grains, and citrus fruits.
B12 (cobalamin) assists in: • metabolism. • functioning of nervous system. • prevention of pernicious anemia. • proper formation of blood cells. • controlling levels of homocysteine, a chemical in the blood that is associated with heart attacks, strokes, and blood clots when it is elevated.	Vitamin B12 is not found in significant quantities in plant food. Best sources for vegetarians include yogurt as well as fortified almond milk, fortified coconut milk, dairy milk, and eggs.

Vitamin C

This water-soluble vitamin is a powerful antioxidant. It has long been used to prevent the onset of colds and flu, but recent research suggests it may reduce the duration of such illnesses rather than prevent them. Of most interest perhaps is its role in helping to prevent certain cancers. It appears that low levels of vitamin C are associated with an increased risk of various cancers, particularly those of the mouth, stomach, esophagus, pancreas, and cervix. Deficiencies also cause scurvy.

Vitamin C supports: • natural immunity. • healthy gums, teeth, and bones. • wound-healing. • iron absorption.	Good plant sources of vitamin C include bell peppers, leafy green vegetables (kale, spinach), kiwifruit, broccoli, berries, citrus fruits, papaya, and melons (cantaloupe, honeydew).

Vitamin D

Vitamin D is a fat-soluble vitamin that is produced by the body through exposure to sunlight. It is not possible to source adequate vitamin D from food, hence the frequent use of vitamin D supplements through the winter months. Low vitamin D levels appear to be linked to several diseases. It is not clear whether some deficiencies arise as a result of specific diseases, or vice versa. In particular, its possible roles in preventing certain cancers, boosting the immune system, and treating and preventing depression are the subject of ongoing research.

Vitamin D:
- assists in bone formation.
- boosts absorption of calcium and phosphorous.
- helps guard against osteoporosis and rickets.

Vitamin D is produced by the skin through exposure to UV rays in sunlight, although small amounts are found in some foods such as UV-irradiated mushrooms and fortified margarines.

Vitamin E

Vitamin E is a fat-soluble vitamin and an antioxidant that is being researched specifically for its possible role in preventing cancer and heart disease. Vitamin E has also long been used in topical treatments to assist in wound-healing and the treatment of scars, but as yet there is no scientific evidence in support of these claims.

Vitamin E:
- supports the immune system.
- is a powerful antioxidant.
- is undergoing continuing research regarding its possible role in helping to prevent cancer and heart disease.

Good plant sources of vitamin E include nuts (almonds, hazelnuts, pistachios, pecans, walnuts), seeds (sunflower, pumpkin, sesame), avocados, and olive oil.

Vitamin K

Vitamin K is fat-soluble vitamin. It is produced in the body by intestinal bacteria and is also found in some foods.

Vitamin K:
- assists in helping the blood to clot.

Good plant sources of vitamin K include herbs (parsley, basil, chives, water-cress), green leafy vegetables (spinach, collard greens, broccoli rabe), romaine lettuce, celery, cucumbers, broccoli, fennel, and prunes.

Minerals are essential for regulating water balance and enabling chemical reactions to occur in the body, and they also form the hard structures of the body. Of the many minerals found in food and utilized by the body, fourteen of the most important are described in these tables.

Calcium	
Calcium assists in: • bone formation and strength. • nerve and muscle function. • blood pressure control. • weight control.	Good plant sources of calcium are milk, yogurt, cheese, nuts, seeds, green leafy vegetables, fortified breads, soy products, and fruit juices.

Chromium	
Chromium: • is important for normal growth. • assists the action of insulin. • helps to control blood glucose level.	Good plant sources of chromium include broccoli, barley, oats, green beans, tomatoes, and black pepper.

Copper	
Copper: • is an important component of enzymes. • has a role in red blood cell production and nervous system function.	Good plant sources of copper include kale, mushrooms, sesame seeds, nuts, prunes, and avocados.

Fluoride	
Fluoride: • is important for strong bones and teeth. • protects against tooth decay. • may protect against osteoporosis.	The main source is fluoridated water. Plant sources include green beans, celery, and radishes.

Iodine	
Iodine is needed for: • thyroid function. • energy metabolism.	Best sources include iodized salt and seaweed. Plant sources include green beans, bananas, and strawberries.

Iron	
Iron: • helps form hemoglobin. • prevents anemia. • assists cognitive function and motor development. • boosts immunity.	Good plant sources of iron include cacao, dried fruit, dark leafy green vegetables, whole grains, legumes, nuts, and seeds.

Magnesium

Magnesium is needed for: • growth and maintenance of bones. • functioning of nerves, muscles, and many other parts of the body. • neutralizing stomach acid and moving stools through the intestine.	Good plant sources of magnesium include dark leafy green vegetables, whole grains, and avocados.

Manganese

Manganese is needed for: • enzyme activation.	Good plant sources of manganese include dark leafy green vegetables, whole grains, nuts, seeds, kale, and spinach.

Molybdenum

Molybdenum: • contributes to the use of iron in the body. • assists in metabolism of waste.	Good plant sources of molybdenum include legumes, whole grains, and tomatoes.

Phosphorous

Phosphorous is important for: • the formation of bones and teeth. • the body's use of carbohydrates and fats. • the growth, maintenance, and repair of cells and body tissues. • the body's storing of energy. • kidney function. • maintaining normal heartbeat. • proper nerve signaling. • muscle contractions.	Good plant sources of phosphorous include seeds (chia, sesame, pumpkin), Brazil nuts, and lentils. Low-fat dairy products are also a good source.

Potassium

Potassium helps: • muscles to contract. • maintain fluid balance in the body and a normal blood pressure. • maintain regular heartbeat.	Good plant sources of potassium include white (cannellini) beans, dark leafy green vegetables, dried apricots, mushrooms, bananas, and avocados.

Selenium

Selenium: • has an important role in metabolism.	Good plant sources of selenium include Brazil nuts, lima beans, seeds (flax, sunflower, sesame, chia), broccoli, cabbage, and spinach.

Sodium

Sodium:

- is used by the body to control blood pressure and blood volume.
- helps muscles and nerves to function properly.

Good plant sources of sodium include the tropical mammee apple, guavas, passion fruit, cardoons, celeriac, artichokes, beets, carrots, and celery.

Zinc

Zinc:

- is needed for the body's immune system to work properly.
- plays a role in cell division and wound-healing.
- has a role in the metabolism of carbohydrates.
- is needed for the senses of smell and taste.
- helps the body to grow properly.

Good plant sources of zinc include spinach, pumpkin seeds, and cacao.

Carbohydrates

The main role of carbohydrates is to provide energy to the body. They come mainly from plants, including fruits, starchy vegetables, grains, and legumes. Although fats and proteins can also be used for energy, carbohydrates are the primary source.

Carbohydrates are broken down to glucose before being absorbed into the bloodstream. Glucose then circulates in the blood, providing fuel to the brain, and energy to the body and muscles, among other things. Importantly, not all carbohydrates are broken down by the body at the same rate. Those that break down more slowly are said to have a "low-glycemic index" or "low GI."

The GI level in foods is classified into three groups. Low-GI foods have a GI of 55 or less, intermediate-GI foods have a GI between 55 and 70, and high-GI foods have a GI of 70 or above.

Low GI foods are healthier than high GI foods for a number of reasons. In particular, they provide a steady but slow release of glucose into the bloodstream that results in smaller fluctuations in blood glucose and insulin levels. This in turn helps sustain energy over longer periods and also helps control appetite while promoting feelings of satiety and fullness for longer. These have obvious implications for weight management, but also in a wide range of other areas, such as helping to alleviate mood swings and to treat conditions such as diabetes and hyperglycemia.

Many fruits and some starchy vegetables are marvelous sources of low-GI carbohydrates, providing high-quality, slow release energy. Their fiber content also helps to make you feel full and staves off hunger for longer.

Protein

The main role of protein is to build, maintain, and repair our bodies. The amino acids found in proteins are called the "building blocks" of our bodies. When protein is digested, it is broken down into amino acids that are then reassembled in different configurations and

used to rebuild the physical components of the body. Amino acids make up a large portion of our muscles and body tissues, and give structure to cells. Enzymes and other blood compounds are also built from amino acids, and they are essential for the building of bone and cartilage.

There are at least twenty known amino acids, some of which we are able to source from food or produce ourselves, and others that must be sourced through food. Good sources of plant protein, and hence amino acids, include grains, legumes, and nuts. As some are lacking in certain amino acids but not in others, it is worth mixing the different sources of plant proteins so shortfalls in one food are corrected by the amino acids in another. Smoothies provide an ideal way to blend nuts and seeds together with legumes and other ingredients to ensure the body has all the amino acids it needs. The casein found in yogurt is high in amino acids and an ideal addition to smoothies, while non-dairy alternatives such as coconut yogurt and almond milk are also good,

although less rich, protein sources. Some commercially produced soy milks contain all of the essential amino acids.

Fats

There are all kinds of fats, including very good ones and very bad ones. Good fats (and oils, which are liquid fats) are essential for good health and should be included in the diet.

Fat is also a secondary source of energy for the body, after carbohydrates and before proteins. So when the body runs low on carbohydrates, it can source its energy needs from available fat before drawing on protein (which would break down muscles and other protein structures in the body to provide energy). Fat is essential for storing fat-soluble vitamins and other nutrients, and it provides cushioning and insulation to the internal organs. And although this may be an uncommon consideration in privileged, well-sheltered, and well-fed (overweight?) societies, fat is a concentrated source of energy. Fat provides about twice as many calories per ounce as carbohydrates and protein do. This has long been of critical importance to indigenous nomadic people dependent on seasonal availability of food, and to those living in very cold climates and who have a greater need for energy and also fat to both generate and retain warmth in their bodies.

It's widely known that a diet too high in fat will, for most people, result in weight issues and all their attendant problems.

However, it's equally important to understand the relationship between fat and cholesterol, and in turn "good" (high-density lipoprotein, or "HDL") and "bad" (low-density lipoprotein, or "LDL") cholesterol.

First, cholesterol itself is not a fat. It is a waxlike substance that is essential for a number of bodily functions. Some cholesterol is made by the body itself, and other cholesterol is found in food. Generally, if a healthy person consumes too much cholesterol, the body will compensate by either producing less cholesterol of its own or excreting the excess.

Second, confusion arises because it seems that cholesterol is at once both essential and unhealthy. Not so. In fact, cholesterol only becomes a problem when there is too much in the blood, and when that cholesterol is what is known as LDL cholesterol.

LDL cholesterol is unhealthy because it contributes to the build-up of plaque on the artery walls. Plaque is a thick, hard deposit that clogs and hardens arteries, both narrowing them and making them less flexible, and causing a condition known as atherosclerosis. If a clot then forms and blocks an artery, it is likely to result in a stroke or heart attack. Other diseases are also associated with the build-up of plaque in the arteries, such as peripheral artery disease, which

results when narrowing of the arteries reduces the supply of blood to the legs.

On the other hand, HDL cholesterol appears to have a cleansing action, helping to remove LDL from the arteries and transport it back to the liver where it is broken down and then excreted.

Third, as both a preventative and corrective measure, it makes sense to limit the consumption of saturated fat because our livers appear to make LDL cholesterol from saturated fats.

Dietary fats (and oils) are categorized into four different types:

- saturated fats.
- monounsaturated fats.
- polyunsaturated fats (omega-3 and omega-6).
- trans fats.

Saturated Fats: These are found mainly in meat and dairy foods, but also in palm oil and coconut oil. Most fruits and vegetables are very low in saturated fats, with some notable exceptions, such as coconut, which is high in saturated fat, and avocados.

Some saturated fats—not all—contribute to higher levels of "bad" LDL cholesterol, which in turn increases the risk of cardiovascular problems. The link between saturated fat and heart disease is a contentious issue. Some research is suggesting that when saturated fat is found with calcium in foods like dairy products, the effect of the saturated fat may not be as damaging as once thought. Research is also being undertaken to look at the effects of coconut consumption on blood cholesterol levels and plaque formation in the arteries. The research is not yet conclusive, but given that some saturated fats and oils are known to contribute to cholesterol problems, and others seem to be implicated in other serious health disorders, it makes sense to keep consumption of saturated fats to a minimum. Obviously, people with existing heart conditions should avoid them completely. A diet high in fresh fruit and vegetables is less likely to be high in saturated fat, and possibly certain nutrients found in fresh

produce may help to counteract
the adverse effects of some
saturated fats, unless they
are cooked in buttery sauces.

Monounsaturated Fats:
These are high-quality,
good fats that are found mainly
in oils and fats from plant sources, including
olives, avocados, and nuts. Unlike saturated fats, monounsaturated fats help reduce
the levels of LDL cholesterol in the blood—
although less effectively than polyunsaturated
fats—and hence help reduce the risk of heart
and cardiovascular diseases.

Polyunsaturated Omega-6 Fats: These come mainly from plant seeds,
such as sunflower and sesame, and are used to make cooking oils. They
are also found in grains, and are effective in reducing all types of
cholesterol (both LDL and, less fortunately, HDL) in the blood.

Polyunsaturated Omega-3 Fats: These are polyunsaturated fats
that, in addition to being able to reduce the levels of cholesterol
in the blood, are able to thin the blood, reducing its ability to clot.
They therefore have an important role in reducing the risk of heart
and cardiovascular diseases. Omega-3 fats are found in both
seafood and plant foods, with the strongest evidence of benefits
to date being associated with the seafood. Nonetheless, omega-3
fats can be obtained from plant sources, including canola oil,
flaxseed (linseed), chia seeds, and walnuts. Research into the
potential benefits of omega-3 fats is continuing, but indications

are that they have strong anti-inflammatory effects and positive implications in the treatment and prevention of rheumatoid arthritis, inflammatory bowel disease, stroke, hypertension, and depression. They also may boost immunity and reduce overall inflammation.

Trans Fats: These are unsaturated fats that behave like saturated fats and are, therefore, unhealthy. They occur naturally in certain animal foods, including some dairy products as well as beef and lamb, but are not found in fruit, vegetables, or grains—another reason why a diet high in fruit and vegetables is such a healthy option. That said, our bodies have managed the trans fats found in animal foods for centuries without too many problems; the problems are associated more with commercial fats used in food production—for example, liquid vegetable oils that are artificially converted into solids, such as certain margarines. For this reason, it pays to inspect food labels and avoid foods with trans fats as much as possible.

Fiber

Dietary fiber, or "roughage," is the indigestible parts of plant food that pass through the digestive tract and bowel and are eventually eliminated. There are three types: soluble, insoluble, and resistant starch.

Soluble fiber dissolves in water and forms a gel-like substance. It promotes satiety, contributes to the removal of cholesterol from the body, and helps to control blood sugar levels. Pectin, the fiber in fruit, is a soluble fiber, as is the fiber found in legumes. Insoluble fiber is the structural component of the plant found in vegetables and fruit peels and, while also promoting satiety, helps speed the passage of food through the bowel. This is important for a number of reasons, not least because it prevents constipation and reduces the length of time that toxic substances are in contact with the membranes of the bowel.

Resistant starch is a type of fiber that resists digestion and ferments in the large bowel where it produces acids that offer protection against bowel cancer. Certain grains and cold, cooked potatoes are examples of foods high in resistant starch (warmed potatoes are more digestible but their starch becomes less resistant).

Water

Water is both essential and beneficial in more ways than can be listed here. Suffice to say that our bodies—both the rigid and fluid parts and everything in between—are composed mostly of water, and hence it is needed for our very existence. It is required in some way in every bodily function, as well as the more obvious functions of enabling excretion of waste through the kidneys, transporting nutrients around the body in the blood, helping food to pass through the digestive system, aiding thermoregulation, helping to suppress appetite, moistening our eyes and mouths, and keeping our skin plump and nourished. Without water we could not survive.

INGREDIENTS

It is fair to say that there is no one food that can cause or cure disease. With the ever rising popularity of "super foods," it's important to put these highly nutritious foods into perspective when it comes to the prevention and treatment of diseases such as heart disease, cancer, and Alzheimer's disease. One way of looking at it is to acknowledge that some foods are more nutritious than others. When considering a healthy food group like fruit and vegetables, some choices within this group may be richer in a certain vitamin, mineral, phytonutrient, or other component than others. And, even though we can't say that eating fruit and vegetables will cure all the diseases of the modern era, we can say that it may offer us some protection against developing many of these diseases by reducing some of the risk factors.

Variety is of the utmost importance when it comes to the nutritional value of smoothies, so be sure to vary the ingredients as much as you can rather than keeping to "favorites." Experiment with different combinations and see what works for you.

Pages 150–58 provide some additional information on protein supplements, milk alternatives, sweeteners, grains, nuts, and seeds.

Basic Ingredients

Acai

Recently touted by many people as a "super food", this fruit of the acai palm has a large seed and very little flesh. Because it perishes quickly, it is frozen or freeze-dried immediately after picking. It is then used in a variety of health foods, beverages, and supplements. Like all fruit, acai is nutritious, but many of the more amazing claims regarding its "miracle" properties are yet to be proven. As fresh acai is not generally available, its nutritional quality will vary depending on the quality of the product in which it is contained.

Acai is not a berry, as is often thought. Rather, it is a drupe (stone fruit). The association with berries is most likely on account of its small size and deep blue color. Because acai has a slightly bitter rather than sweet flavor, it is generally mixed with fruit juices to improve its taste. Acai contains antioxidants, which can protect the body's cells from free-radical damage, support cardiovascular health, and help to boost the immune system. Antioxidants are also thought to play a role in slowing down the aging process. Acai has high fiber content, is rich in vitamin E, and contains small amounts of calcium and iron.

Alfalfa

Both the seeds and sprouts
of this light, crunchy legume are
a rich source of beta-carotene, a highly
potent antioxidant that the body
also converts to vitamin A. Alfalfa
contains several other minerals
(calcium, iron, magnesium, phosphorous,
and potassium) as well as vitamins B1, B3,
B12, D, C, E, and K.

Fresh alfalfa is readily available in super-
markets and health food stores. It is used in salads
and sandwiches as well as beverages like
smoothies and tea. While it is thought that alfalfa
might assist in the treatment of various health
conditions, most of these claims are still subject
to further study.

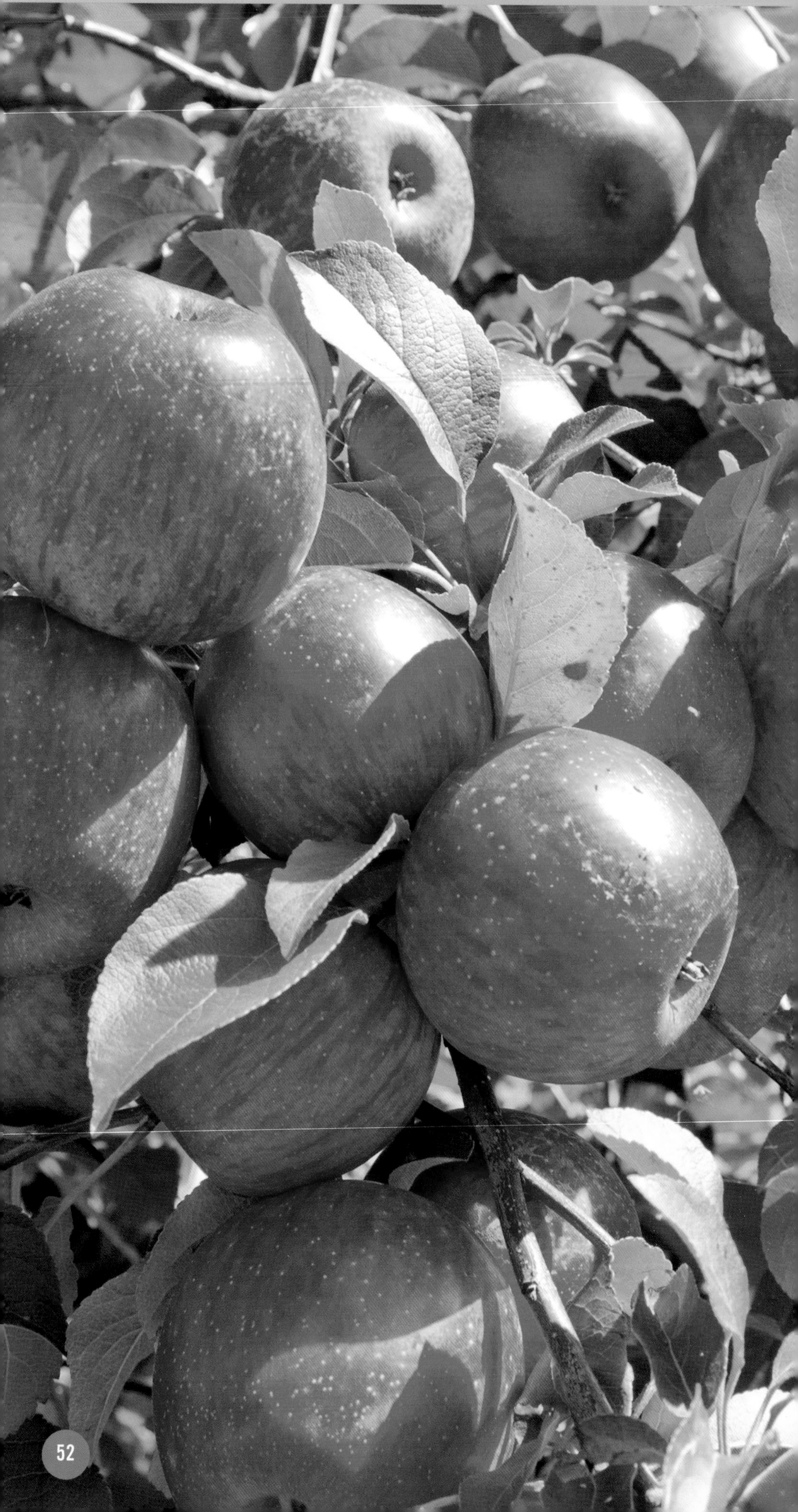

Apple

Perhaps the best-known and most popular of all fruits, apples are remarkably nutritious and versatile. They are full of important nutrients, especially dietary fiber, as well as carbohydrates. They have a low GI (38) and are a source of vitamin C, many of the B-group vitamins (riboflavin, thiamin, and vitamin B6), and various minerals, including calcium and potassium.

Apples are rich in antioxidants, and it is thought that their polyphenols may provide a protective benefit for our lungs and airways. Importantly, apples are high in a fiber called pectin, a gelling agent that offers particular digestive benefits by speeding the passage of food through the digestive tract and hence reducing the time that the mucous membrane of the colon is exposed to toxic substances in the stool. Additionally, pectin plays a role in reducing cholesterol levels. Best of all, apples are widely available year-round, and the high number of varieties means there is always a wide selection of varying flavors from sweet to tart to choose from. Generally, the more green the apple, the more tart the flavor.

Apricot

This delicious stone fruit (a "drupe") has a soft flesh that blends beautifully into smoothies. The flavor is sweet, but has a distinctive tang.

Apricots are very nutritious. Their lovely orange color immediately signals the presence of the antioxidant beta-carotene within. They are also high in vitamin A, potassium, and copper, and have good amounts of vitamin C, calcium, silicon, and phosphorous, among other nutrients. Naturally, they are full of fiber, too. Apricot kernels, however, contain a toxic chemical that the body converts to cyanide, which is poisonous.

Traditionally, apricots have been a popular ingredient in jams, and are also stewed. Dried apricots make a tasty snack, and can be added to smoothies if desired.

Avocado

The rich, smooth flesh of this subtly flavored fruit lends a seductively creamy texture to green smoothies that works particularly well with cacao and banana. Despite the creamy texture, avocados are also high in fiber. They are rich in heart-friendly monounsaturated fats, as well as vitamins C, E, K, beta-carotene, and folate, and the mineral potassium. It is thought that monounsaturated fats in avocados may assist in maintaining good cholesterol and blood sugar levels. Avocados are also a particularly satisfying food that helps to keep hunger at bay for longer periods of time. Adding avocados to smoothies can increase the absorption of carotenoids like beta-carotene from other colorful fruits and vegetables.

Banana

Bananas have many claims to fame, but perhaps they are best known for their high levels of potassium, which along with a low-sodium diet can help keep blood pressure in check.

Bananas are the best fruit source of vitamin B6, which helps with the production of serotonin. They also have small amounts of the other B vitamins, and contain vitamin C. They are low in sodium, make a good source of energy-giving carbohydrates, and have a low GI (52). Unripe bananas are a great source of resistant starch. Widely available, bananas are an ideal ingredient in smoothies due to their creamy texture, sweet flavor, high fiber content, and excellent nutritional value.

Beans

See "Legumes" on page 111.

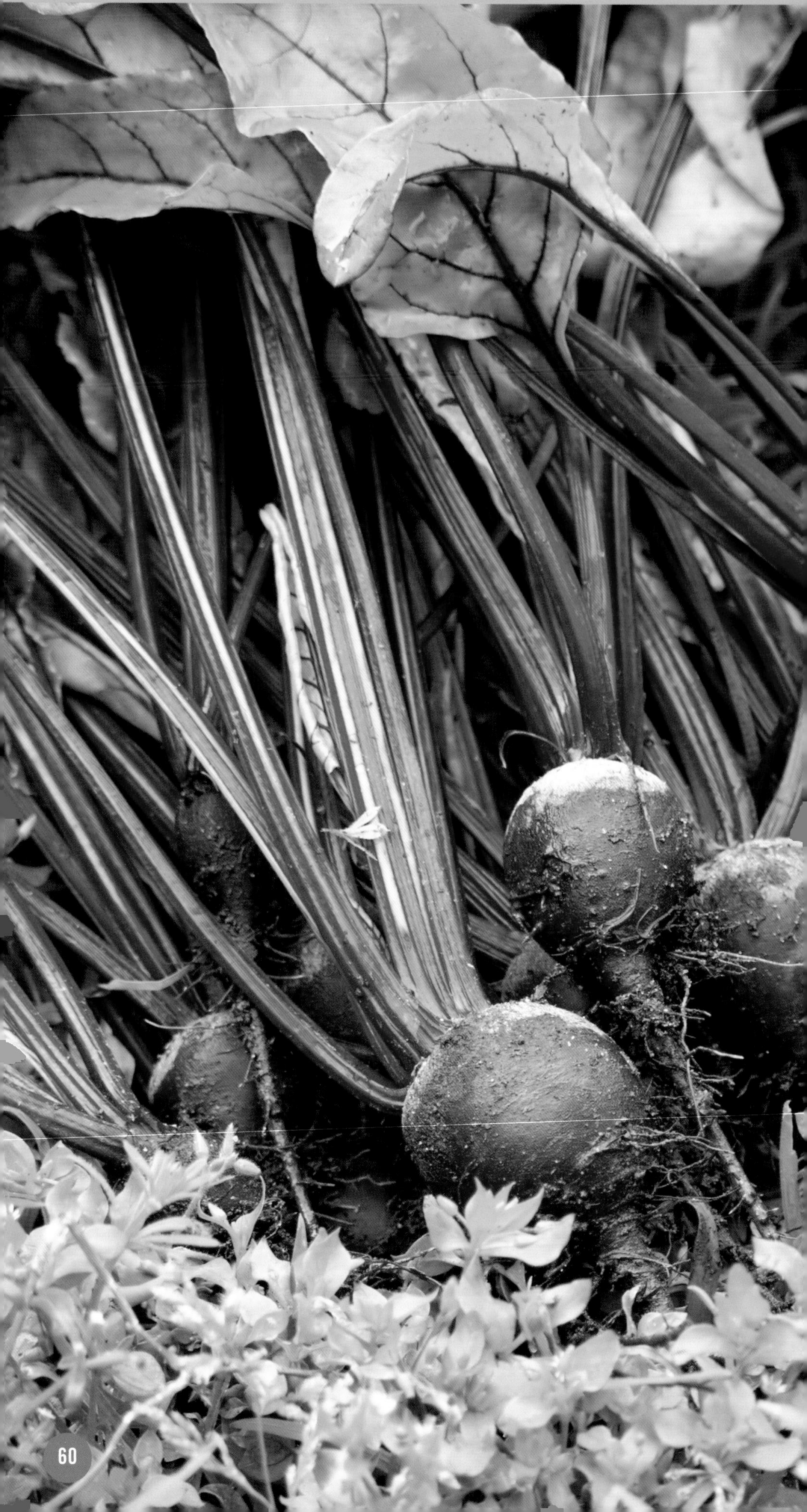

Beet

Beets have two edible parts: the root and the leaves. They have a sweet flavor and come in a variety of colors ranging from garnet red to white. Nutritionally, they are a good source of vitamins A and C, iron, beta-carotene, potassium, calcium, folate, and fiber. The greens contain certain nutrients in higher concentration than in the root, so be sure to eat them or throw them in the smoothie, too. Beets are low in calories and high in a phytonutrient called betaine, which is thought to help lower blood pressure and offer heart health benefits.

Blackberry

This deeply colored berry is rich in vitamin C and has one of the highest antioxidant levels of all fruits. Blackberries are also thought to have certain antiviral, anticarcinogen, and antibacterial agents. They are low in calories and have a tart, sweet flavor.

When buying or picking blackberries, choose ones that are plump, dry, deeply colored, and quite firm to the touch. They are highly perishable, so they should be consumed as soon as possible or refrigerated for up to five days.

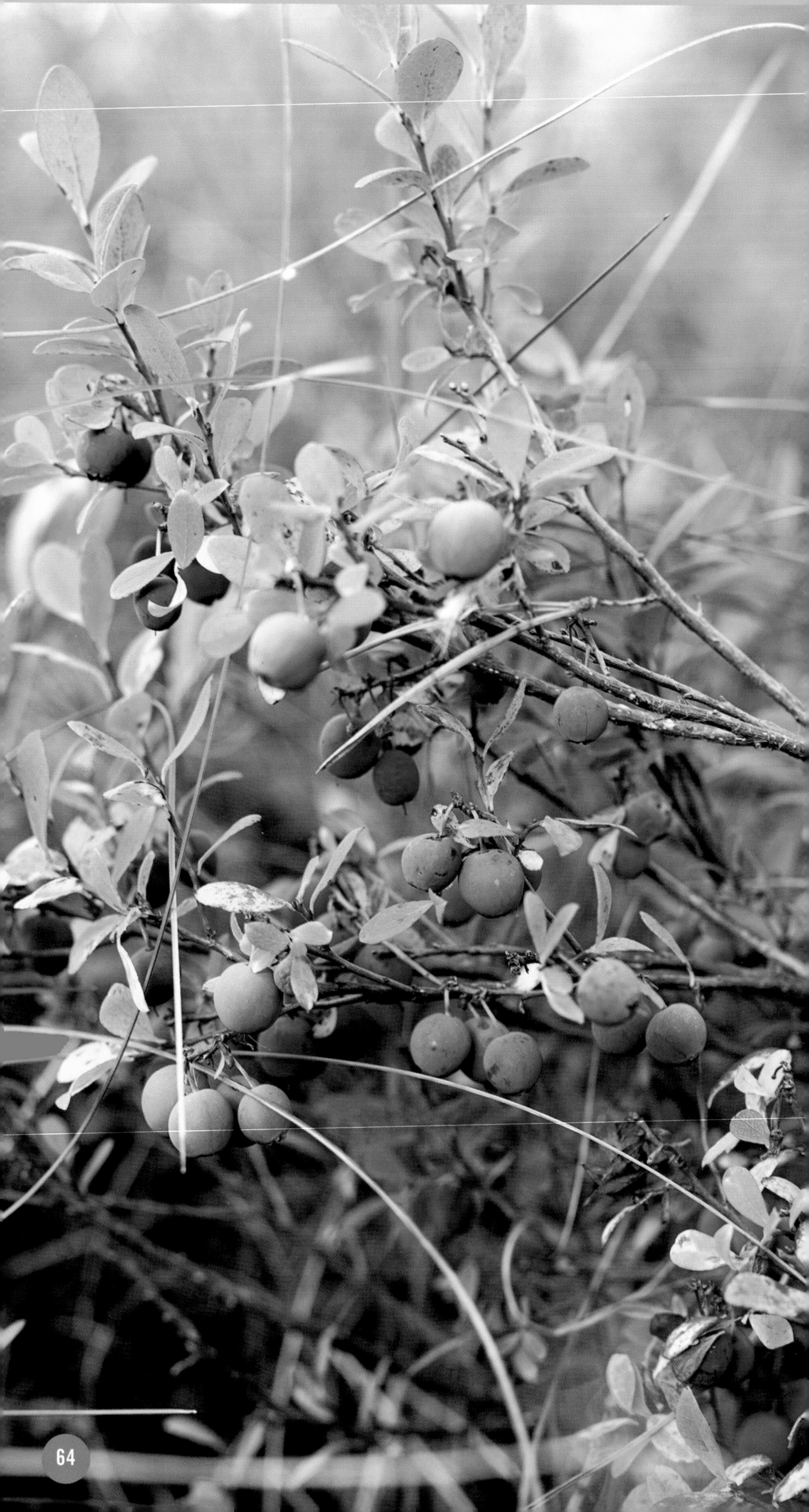

Blueberry

Blueberries are one of the original super foods. They are exceptionally high in the phytonutrients called anthocyanins, found in the blue skin of the berry and the source of the blueberry's antioxidant power. So highly regarded are their antioxidant properties that some health experts have suggested that if you are going to make just one change to your diet—make it the addition of blueberries. Blueberries are nicknamed brain berries because research in rodents has shown improvements in the rodents' cognitive function when they were fed blueberries. The antioxidants in these berries may also be useful in decreasing the risk of Alzheimer's disease and age-related macular degeneration. Like all berries, they are highly perishable, and quickly become "squishy" and begin to lose their nutritional value. Fortunately, studies have shown that blueberries can be frozen for three months without damaging their antioxidant properties. Blueberries have a mild, slightly sweet, slightly tart flavor that is not particularly distinctive but combines well with other fruits.

Broccoli

Broccoli is full of iron, vitamin C, chlorophyll, and sulfur compounds. Sulfur is an important mineral often omitted from nutrition tables—probably because it is widely available in foods. Present in every cell in the human body, it has important roles in insulin function, metabolizing protein, and fighting bacteria. It is also known as the beauty mineral because it helps promote smooth skin, glossy hair, and hard nails.

Broccoli contains an enzyme, myrosinase, that converts some sulfur compounds into other compounds called isothiocyanates, which have anticancer properties. It also contains a specific trio of phytonutrients that work together to assist in detoxification and the elimination of contaminants.

Animal proteins are considered the best dietary sources of sulfur. Vegans and vegetarians may therefore be at greater risk of a deficiency, and so sulfur-rich vegetables have a special role in their diets. Because broccoli is low in calories and high in bulk and fiber, it is also an ideal inclusion in any weight-management plan.

Broccoli Rabe

This variety of broccoli presents small green florets atop its long, leafy stalks. It is a good source of vitamins A and C, among other nutrients. Like broccoli, it is thought to have anticancer properties.

Cabbage

People often dislike cooked cabbage because of its unappealing smell, but raw cabbage has a subtle, fresh scent and a light flavor. In smoothies, it works best when combined with other vegetables and fruit. Nutritionally, cabbage is a rich source of vitamin C, and contains high levels of sulfur together with a number of other minerals. The health benefits of sulfur are gradually attaining increased recognition, and it is thought that cabbage's sulfur-containing compounds called sulphurophanes may play a critical role in detoxification and the treatment of inflammatory conditions. Cabbage is also full of antioxidants that assist in lowering cholesterol and might help prevent certain cancers. Many naturopaths also recommend cabbage in the treatment of constipation and other digestive issues, as well as for alleviating depression.

Cacao

The beans from the cacao tree are most nutritious in their raw form. They may be dried and broken into smaller pieces ("cacao nibs") or ground into a powder. When roasted and ground, the beans are the main component of cocoa. In smoothies, cacao combines brilliantly with smooth fruits, such as bananas and avocados, and sweet fruits like berries. It quickly takes on all the flavors and textures of a luscious and indulgent dessert.

Cacao has a high level of antioxidants called flavonols that benefit heart health by reducing the oxidation of LDL cholesterol. Cacao is also an excellent source of magnesium and provides trace amounts of other minerals, including calcium, chromium, copper, iron, potassium, sulfur, and zinc.

Caffeine-like substances in cacao can provide an energy boost, while other compounds assist in the production of serotonin, the "feel-good hormone," and so may help to improve mood and reduce anxiety. Like its cousin chocolate, cacao is quite high in fat and should be used in moderation; on the flipside, there is some evidence to suggest that the chromium in cacao may assist in stabilizing blood sugar and reducing appetite.

Carob

Carob comes from the pods of the carob tree. It is high in antioxidants and various other nutrients. Raw carob powder is now readily available in many health stores and is said to have a smoother, richer flavor than roasted carob. Carob has traditionally been used as a chocolate or cocoa substitute (because it does not have caffeine or theobrine, the stimulants in cocoa), but it nonetheless has an appetizing taste of its own that is naturally less bitter than cocoa. Combined with various other ingredients the flavor becomes very chocolate-like.

Cantaloupe

See "Melons" on
page 120.

Carrot

Carrots range in color from deep blues and purples to orange and red to yellow and cream; their colors alone are an indicator of their high nutrient value. The plant pigment beta-carotene, a phyto-nutrient in carrots, is responsible for their delightful red-orange-yellow colors, while the blue-purple varieties contain another pigment, anthocyanin. Both are powerful antioxidants. Beta-carotene, for example, assists in the prevention of age-related macular degeneration, the leading cause of blindness in people over 50 years of age. It is also converted by the body to vitamin A, which has a critical role in maintaining eye health and healthy skin. Carrots contain many other carotenoids like lutein, also vitally important for protecting against macular degeneration. Carrots are low in calories and high in fiber, and their slightly sweet taste can be used to enhance the flavor of less palatable vegetables.

Celery

Celery has a lovely, fresh, slightly peppery taste that
helps to lift the flavor of vegetable smoothies but also
combines beautifully with fruits like pears and apples
to produce light, refreshing beverages. It is especially
rich in potassium and is also a source of vitamins A,
C, K, and folate, as well as phosphorous and sodium.
Some studies have found that compounds in celery
known as phthalides are capable of reducing high
blood pressure, but it is not yet clear whether the
consumption of everyday amounts of celery would
deliver sufficient phthalides to be effective. It
does seem likely that future research will establish
clear links between cardiovascular health and the
phthalides found in celery.

Cherry

These delicious little fruits are a type of drupe (stone fruit) and are packed with nutrients and antioxidants. Their deep red/purple color is derived from pigments known as anthocyanins, which are also powerful antioxidants. These anthocyanins have been shown to have anti-inflammatory properties, and may assist in the treatment of arthritis and other related disorders. Indeed, folk medicine has traditionally used cherries in the management of osteoarthritis, rheumatoid arthritis, and gout. Cherries also have an important role in the production of collagen, the protein that holds our body together and supports the skin. It is thought that the antioxidants in cherries may have anti-aging properties—from the brain cells right down to the skin.

There are several varieties of cherries, of which the "wild" or "sweet-cherry" and the "sour" or "tart cherry" are the most popular. The darker-skinned sour varieties are thought to have greater health benefits, though all are low-calorie and nutritious. Cherries are also a natural source of melatonin, a neurohormone that has long been linked to sleep regulation.

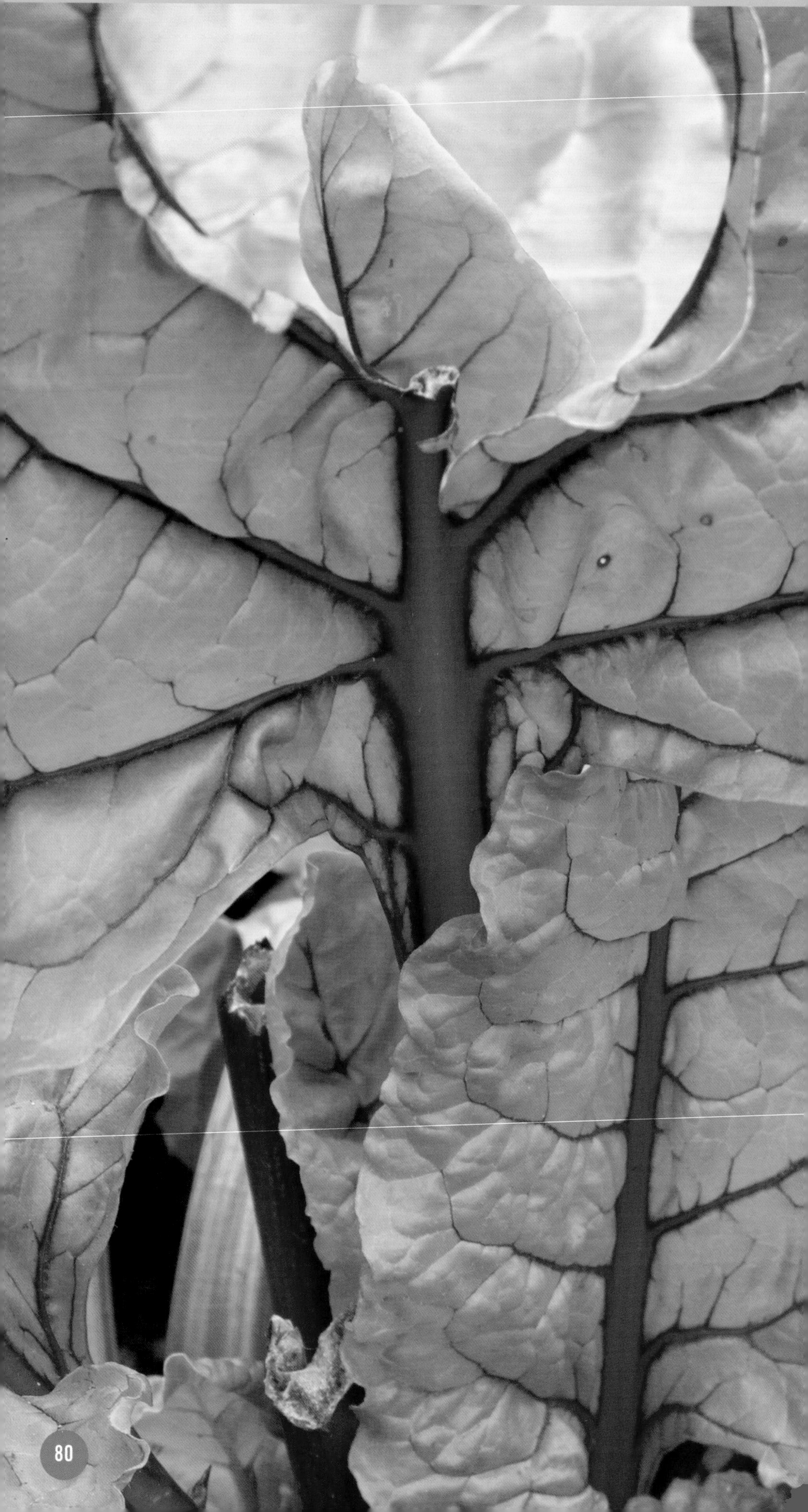

Collard Greens

There are several varieties of
collard greens. Related to kale and
cabbage, the collard plant is low in
calories and exceptionally nutritious.
The leaves are rich in vitamin C,
beta-carotene, lutein, and vitamin K,
as well as many of the B-group vitamins,
including folate. Collard greens also contain
good amounts of soluble fiber, which can
decrease cholesterol absorption, help to
prevent constipation, and assist with overall
bowel function. Certain sulfur compounds
found in collard greens may help protect
against some cancers. The leaves and stems
are both good sources of various minerals
including iron, calcium, and copper.

Cranberry

Cranberries are another fruit rich in antioxidants, particularly anthocyanins, the pigments that give them their deep, rich red and blue colors. Cranberries are also a good source of vitamin C, copper, and fiber, among other nutrients. Some preliminary research indicates that cranberries may be helpful in preventing urinary tract infections, but the findings are not yet conclusive.

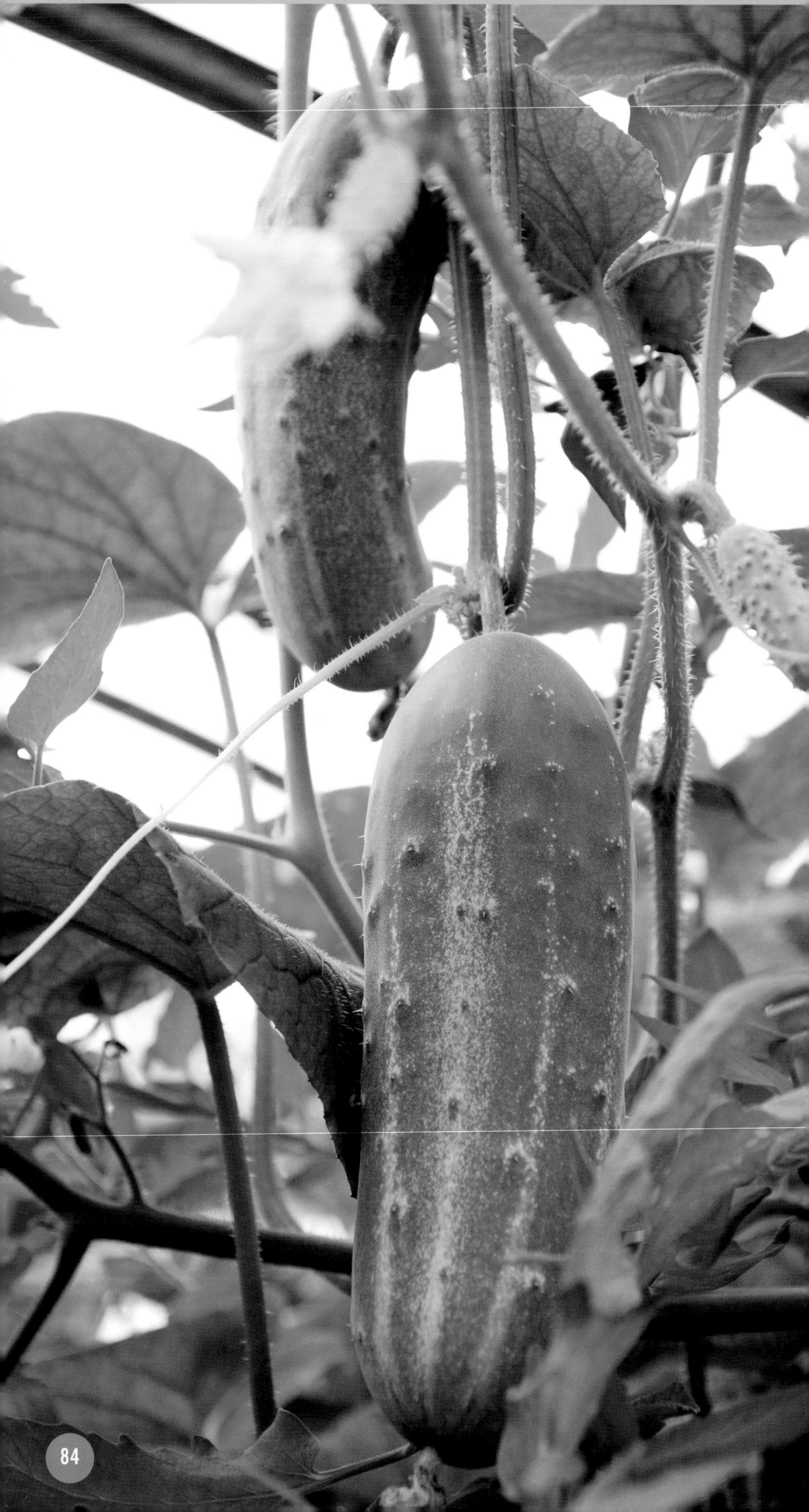

Cucumber

A cousin of zucchini, melons, and squash, this watery vegetable is low in calories and a good inclusion for those wanting to manage their weight. Cucumbers are thought to have anti-inflammatory properties and can be very soothing when applied topically to the skin. Eating cucumbers with the skin provides several beneficial nutrients, including dietary fiber and vitamins K and C.

Cucumber has a crisp, refreshing flavor that works well on its own but also combines well with other fruits and vegetables.

Date

Dates are the fruit of the date palm tree. They provide a delicious sweetness when blended into a smoothie, and also loads of fiber. However, because they are high in calories and fructose, they should be used in moderation. Most varieties except for the medjool date are available only in dried form.

Dates are highly nutritious, and an excellent source of iron and potassium. They also provide vitamins A and K as well as the B-group vitamins. They are rich in antioxidants such as beta-carotene; tannins, which are anti-inflammatory and anti-infective; and lutein and zeaxanthin, which are thought to protect against age-related macular degeneration.

Fennel

This delicious vegetable is the shape of a large bulb, formed by swollen leaf stems. Its straight celery-like stalks are topped with feathery fronds. It has a sweet yet pungent aniseed flavor. Originally from the Mediterranean, it is known in Italy as "finocchio," which, rather sweetly, rhymes with "Pinocchio." The essential oils in fennel are thought to have antifungal and antibacterial properties, and may also assist in digestion. Teas made from the seeds and roots are sometimes used to suppress appetite as well as relieve flatulence.

Fennel is a good source of vitamin C and also provides some vitamin A, folate, and potassium. It blends well with apples, oranges, and other fruits, and forms a particularly intriguing flavor when paired with cilantro.

Garlic

This pungently flavored bulb has long been used in the preparation of both food and herbal medicines and is commonly referred to as "nature's penicillin." Garlic is high in sulfur-containing compounds that are thought to boost immunity and also have antibacterial and antifungal properties; however the most convincing studies relate to garlic and cardiovascular disease. Consumption of garlic has been associated with a reduction in total cholesterol, LDL cholesterol, and triglycerides. An intake between one half and one glove of garlic per day can reduce cholesterol levels by 9 percent. It seems that garlic can lower blood pressure and may also thin the blood and reduce clotting.

Garlic contains a variety of beneficial phytonutrients, one of which is the active component allicin. Raw garlic is higher in allicin than cooked garlic, and preliminary research suggests it may assist in the prevention of stomach and colon cancer.

Ginger

The root of the ginger plant has long been used, in powdered or grated form, as a culinary spice and in various tea infusions. It has an intriguing sweet, peppery, sharp taste that adds a zing to any beverage or culinary dish. It lends itself to both sweet and savory combinations, mixing beautifully with cacao for a sweet treat and just as well with garlic and chili pepper. It is claimed that ginger is a stimulant that relieves flatulence, clears the nasal passages, strengthens digestion, and eases nausea and vomiting. It is also commonly used to prevent motion sickness, especially when at sea.

Gingerol, one of the many phytonutrients in ginger, is thought to have anti-inflammatory effects, and research has shown positive effects of ginger consumption on reducing osteoarthritic pain.

Ginger is low in calories and provides modest amounts of essential vitamins like vitamin C and B6, and minerals including manganese, magnesium, and potassium.

Goji Berry

Also known as wolfberries, goji berries are highly nutritious and contain surprisingly high levels of protein and iron, together with a wide range of other vitamins and minerals. They also have antioxidant properties and have long been used in traditional Chinese medicine to treat various conditions including kidney disorders, diabetes, and high cholesterol. At this stage, the medical research into the touted health benefits is inconclusive, and it is likely that some of the more miraculous claims are overstated.

Nonetheless, these delicious little berries are undoubtedly nutritious and a good source of dietary fiber, and their unusually sweet-and-sour flavor adds an interesting touch to smoothie combinations. Dried goji berries are generally more readily available than fresh.

Grape

The fruit of the grapevine is a rich source of phytonutrients with antioxidant properties. One of these, resveratrol, is found in the skin of red grapes and is thought to have cardiovascular benefits. It may also prevent the development of certain cancers and liver disorders. Grapes also contain the antioxidants lutein and zeaxanthin, which are important for eye health, as well as myricetin and quercetin, which help the body to prevent free radicals from forming.

Grapes have a high water content and are useful for hydration. They are also high in potassium and dietary fiber and contain small amounts of other vitamins and minerals. Deliciously sweet, grapes are a natural way to sweeten smoothies, but because a high portion of their calories is derived from sugars, they should be used in moderation.

Grapefruit

As a citrus fruit, grapefruit is very high in vitamin C, contains a lot of potassium and vitamin B1, and has small amounts of other vitamins and minerals. Both the ruby and pink varieties contain lycopene, a phytonutrient thought to offer some protection against prostate cancer. It has long had a reputation as a "slimming food," with the half-a-grapefruit-for-breakfast regime a popular dieting practice that dates back to the 1960s. Grapefruit, like all citrus fruits, contains soluble fiber, which can help stabilize blood sugar levels and stave off hunger—both useful for weight management.

Grapefruit's juiciness and fresh, uplifting flavor combines well in smoothies with other citrus fruits and melons, and with herbs such as mint. Use the full fruit (except the peel and seeds) in order to retain the benefits of extra fiber and bulk as well as nutrition in the pith and pulp. The pith can add a bitter but not unpleasant flavor, and zest from the peel can be used as a nutritious garnish that also provides freshness, color, and zing. Keep in mind, however, that grapefruit and grapefruit juice can interact with certain medications, so be sure to discuss any concerns you may have with your medical practitioner.

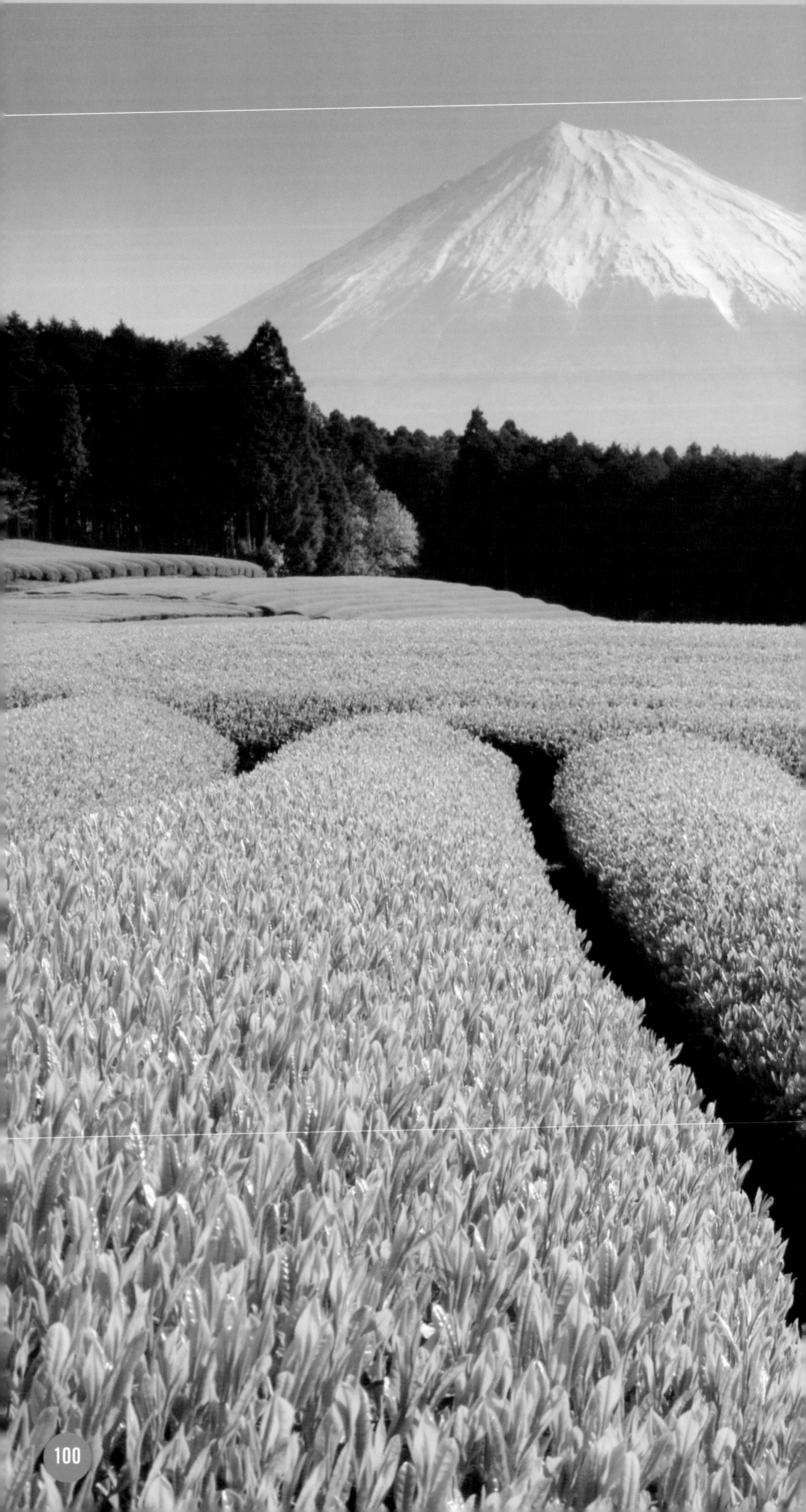

Green Tea

The green tea leaf is the same as a black tea leaf that hasn't yet been oxidized. Green tea offers many health benefits, and has been proven to help prevent heart disease by decreasing inflammation. Phytonutrients in green tea might protect against certain cancers. It is renowned for its antioxidant properties, which stem from its flavonols called catechins. It is likely these are responsible for most of its health-giving benefits.

Green tea is the favorite drink of the people of Okinawa in Japan, which also happens to have the world's highest percentage of centenarians; there may well be a link between these two observations. When used in smoothies, green tea is first brewed, strained, and cooled before it is added to the blend. The tea should be quite strong, but should not be left to brew too long, as it will become bitter. The brew has no calories and is a terrific way to add nutritious fluids, particularly if a lighter, more refreshing and hydrating beverage is desired. It has a subtle flavor that works well with herbs like mint but also combines well with almost all fruits and vegetables. For convenience, green tea can be prepared in advance and frozen into ice cubes, ready to add to smoothies when needed.

Herbs

The list of available herbs and their health and culinary benefits are endless. Nearly all are suitable for smoothies, but here are the most readily available and popular. They are each used dry, fresh, or in infusions, and are all low in calories. In the past, they were used only to enhance the flavor of other foods, but we now know they are also very high in antioxidants—in fact, adding a handful of fresh herbs to a smoothie can enhance its antioxidant capacity by 200 percent!

Basil is an excellent source of vitamins C, K, and A, as well as manganese, copper, iron, and other nutrients. Its particular antioxidants include compounds known as rosmarinic and caffeic acids, as well as beta-carotene. Basil has a deliciously sweet yet peppery flavor.

Basil

Chamomile has long been used for its calming effect, as well as to help ease various digestive conditions and insomnia. It has an unusual subtle yet earthy flavor that is improved if sweetened with a small amount of honey. Chamomile also appears

Chamomile flowers

to have some antibacterial and anti-inflammatory properties. Unfortunately, only limited research into the health benefits of chamomile has been conducted to date, so most of the claims are yet to be proven conclusively. Chamomile tea is made by brewing the leaves in boiling water, which is then strained and consumed. It should be cooled before being added to smoothies.

Cilantro is rich in essential oils and antioxidants, including beta-carotene and vitamin C. It contains many B-group vitamins, including folate, as well as vitamins K and A. It has a uniquely fresh, sweet, yet piquant flavor and can be used as both an ingredient or garnish for smoothies.

Cilantro

Mint is available in many varieties, of which peppermint is perhaps the most common and well known. Its cool, sweet, and refreshing flavor works equally well with both savory and sweet foods and beverages. It is an excellent source of vitamins A and C, and also includes many B-group vitamins. Exceptionally rich in iron and manganese, it is also a very good source of copper, magnesium, and calcium. Mint is high in antioxidants and contains essential oils such as menthol, which is responsible for its cooling flavor and properties.

Mint

Parsley, both the flat- and curly-leaf varieties, can work as a diuretic to flush unwanted water and salt from the body, and theoretically may assist in the treatment of kidney disorders, high blood pressure, and water retention— although the amounts needed may well exceed the usual intake. Parsley is rich in antioxidants (such as beta-carotene and vitamins A and C) and some B-group vitamins like folate. It is exceptionally rich in vitamin K and is a good source of various minerals, including potassium, calcium, iron, and magnesium. To absorb the iron from parsley, it is important that you combine it with a food containing vitamin C.

Parsley

Watercress has a light peppery flavor and according to some research is the most nutrient dense of all foods. Of particular note is its exceptionally high levels of vitamin K, which has an established role in the treatment and prevention of degenerative conditions such as Alzheimer's disease. Watercress contains high levels of antioxidants, including beta-carotene, lutein, zeaxanthin, and vitamins A, C, and E, which together assist in the prevention of cancer and inflammatory diseases and are important for eye health. It is also a good source of B-group vitamins, potassium, and various other minerals.

Watercress

Kale

Kale, a member of the cabbage family, is a particularly nutritious leafy green vegetable. It is high in antioxidants, including beta-carotene, and rich in vitamins A, C, some B-group vitamins like folate, and especially vitamin K. It has high levels of chlorophyll and potassium, and is a good source of various minerals, including copper, iron, and calcium. The powerful combination of carotenoids in kale are thought to assist in lowering the risk of a wide range of disorders, including certain cancers and cardiovascular conditions, while also promoting healthy eyes, skin, and bones and general good health. Kale has a strong, peppery flavor which tends toward bitter, so it tastes best when blended with other vegetables and fruits. This, together with washing, will help minimize the pungent and sometimes mildly unpleasant odor that kale is known to emit.

Kiwifruit

Also known as the Chinese gooseberry, this fruit originated in China but was later cultivated in New Zealand, where it was affectionately given the name of the national bird, the kiwi. Kiwifruit is similar in size and shape to an egg, although covered in a thin, brown, fuzzy peel that conceals the luscious emerald green or gold flesh and tiny black seeds within. The flesh has a slightly wet texture, a little like partially-set jelly, and has a deliciously sweet, uplifting flavor that tastes something like a blend of banana and pineapple. The peel has a mild earthy flavor. Both the peel and seeds contain dietary fiber, while the seeds provide small amounts of ALA, the plant source of omega-3 fatty acids. Gold kiwifruit contains high amounts of lutein and zeaxanthin, which can help protect against macular degeneration. Furthermore, studies in Norway have shown that eating two to three kiwifruits per day can help thin the blood and reduce the risk of blood clots. The kiwifruit is also thought to assist in treating a host of other disorders, including mood imbalances, respiratory problems, and diabetes; research is not yet conclusive, but indications are very positive. The kiwifruit is also exceptionally high in the antioxidant vitamin C, as well as potassium and fiber.

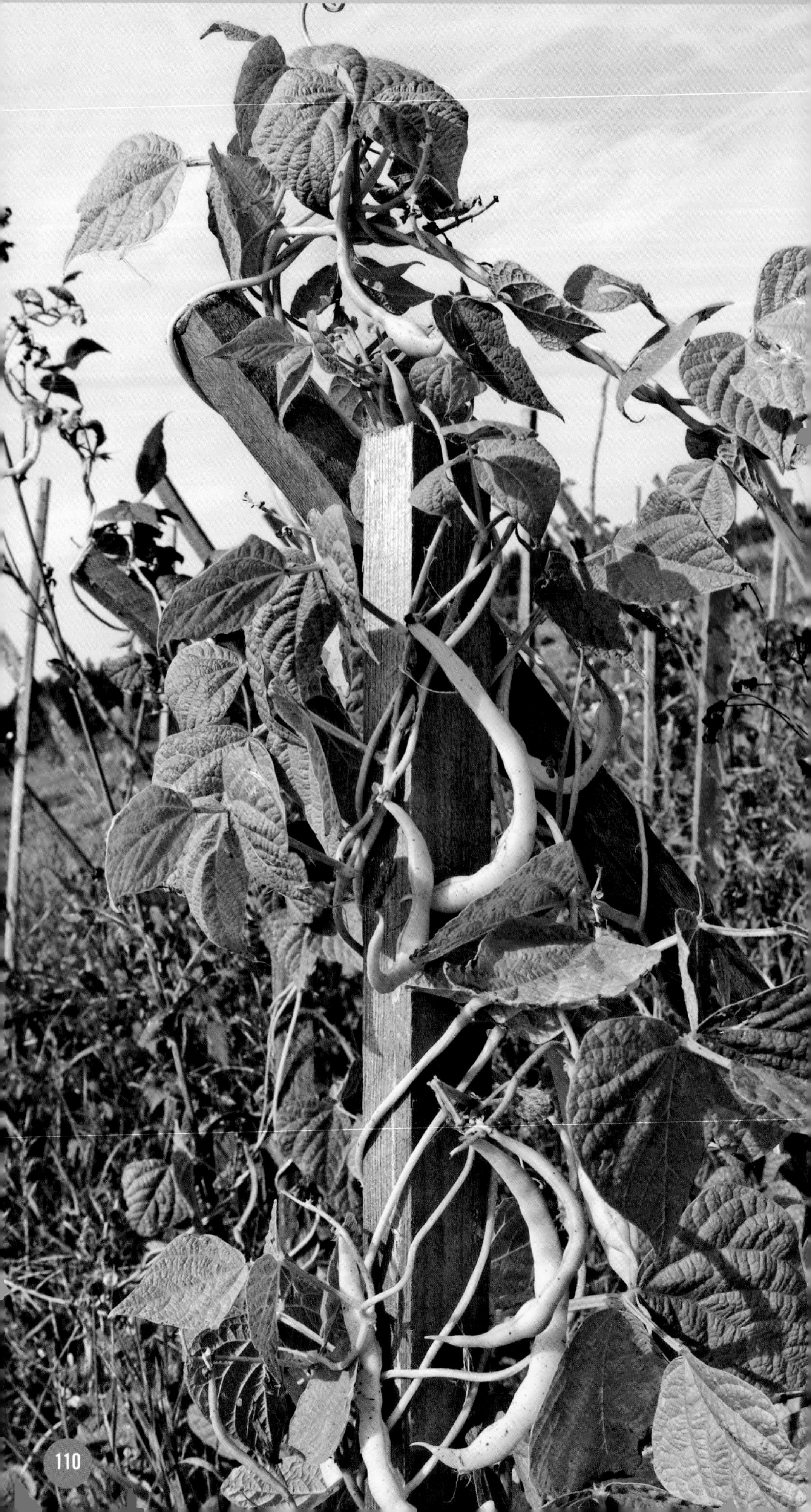

Legumes

Legumes are a type of plant that house their fruit inside a pod. They include all types of beans (such as French beans, kidney beans, soy beans, mung beans, and cannellini beans), peas (including green peas and chickpeas), lentils, and, surprisingly, peanuts. They are highly nutritious, providing both low-GI carbohydrates and protein, together with a host of vitamins and minerals like calcium, potassium, iron, B-group vitamins, and vitamin C. Their high levels of protein make them especially important in vegetarian and vegan diets.

A few legumes can easily be slipped into a fruit-based smoothie to boost the protein and fiber content without affecting flavor. Cannellini beans (also known as white beans or white kidney beans) add a delicious creaminess that blends well with banana without altering taste. Green peas have a light, slightly nutty flavor that will be imperceptible when mixed with more strongly flavored fruits and vegetables, but conversely complements certain flavors such as avocado very nicely. Alfalfa is also considered a legume (see page 50).

Lemon and Lime

Lemons are an excellent source of vitamin C (they have double that of the average orange) and also contain small amounts of various minerals, including calcium, phosphorous, iron, and potassium. Most varieties have a bitter or sour taste that can be sweetened by adding a small amount of raw honey or by mixing with sweeter citrus juices such as orange. The Meyer is thought to be a cross between a lemon and an orange or mandarin, and has a naturally sweet flavor. Lemons can assist in weight management because they are low in calories, high in fiber and also have a low GI. The citric acid in lemon juice slows the rate of digestion and when added to a food or meal can reduce its GI score.

Limes are also a citrus fruit and are related to lemons. Overall, they offer quite similar nutritional benefits. Both are low in calories and are an excellent source of vitamin C. The flavor of lime is slightly sweeter than that of lemons.

Lettuce

A popular salad vegetable, lettuce comes in a number of varieties and colors from light green leaves to dark green leaves tinged with purple. Lettuce is a good source of vitamins A and C, as well as chlorophyll, iron, potassium, and silicon. The darker-leafed varieties tend to be more nutritious. Lettuce leaves contain a substance known as lactucarium, which is, among other things, a natural sedative.

Lime

See "Lemon and Lime" on page 112.

Maca

A cousin of the radish, maca looks something like a small parsnip or turnip and has a nutty, slightly sweet flavor. It is best added to smoothies in liquid or powdered form; a teaspoon, which has only about ten calories, is sufficient. Higher quantities are not generally recommended—maca is known to have certain nontoxic side effects that may nonetheless disturb other processes within the body. Many health practitioners recommend that it be taken in cycles of week on/week off, rather than continually. This can both prevent the body from becoming immune to its benefits and provide a way to assess the body's response to it.

Maca has a high number of nutrients, including B-group vitamins, vitamin C, zinc, calcium, and fatty acids, and hence it supports general good health. There are numerous other claims regarding the health benefits of maca but as yet there is insufficient evidence to confirm them conclusively— although they do sound promising. Supposedly, maca can boost energy, boost sex drive, increase fertility in men and women, relieve migraines, relieve stress, improve memory, and boost immunity, among other things.

Mango

The orange flesh of this delicious drupe
(stone fruit) has a soft, juicy
texture, appealing aroma,
and deliciously sweet taste.
Mangoes are particularly rich in
the antioxidant vitamin C, and are
a good source of vitamins A, E,
potassium, iron, and copper. They also
contain high levels of antioxidants like
beta-carotene and beta cryptoxanthin. Recent
research suggests that mangoes may offer
protection against diabetes, may help reduce
cholesterol, and may even fight breast cancer.
Mangoes blend beautifully with bananas, berries,
and other fruits, and can also add a sweet touch to
more savory blends. They are fiber-rich, and hence
good for digestion and also for promoting satiety.

Melons

Melons come in an array of colors and sizes and are a colorful way to add nutritious liquids to smoothies. Two of the most popular are cantaloupe (rock melon) and watermelon. Both have a high water content (upwards of 90 percent) and are low in calories. The seeds are edible, but are usually scooped out prior to eating. Nutritionally, they are both excellent sources of vitamin A and other antioxidants, and also contain moderate amounts of B-group vitamins and some minerals, particularly copper and potassium.

Cantaloupes have a sweet taste and slightly musky aroma. The flesh ranges in color from soft peach tones to orange; the texture is quite soft compared to other melons, but can be crisp when unripe.

Watermelon has a light, sweet taste and aroma. The flesh is pink and crisp, but quickly becomes watery. Notably, watermelon is a good source of lycopene, a powerful antioxidant that is thought to be even more effective than beta-carotene at combating free radicals in the body.

Orange

This delicious fruit has long been praised for its high quantities of the antioxidant vitamin C and for its energy-giving sugars— hence its juice has traditionally accompanied breakfast.

Oranges are also a good source of vitamin A and several of the B-group vitamins like folate, as well as potassium and other minerals. Foods high in vitamin C help your body to absorb iron, so it's always a good idea to blend them with iron-rich green leafy vegetables. Oranges are much more nutritious, however, when blended whole into a smoothie (without the seeds and peel) rather than juiced, because the fiber is retained and also because the white pith is a source of antioxidants. The fiber in the pith contains pectin, a type of soluble fiber that is also a natural gelling substance used to set jam. Pectin helps to protect the bowel from disease (see pages 44–45) and also helps to reduce cholesterol levels. Even the peel contains phytonutrients (called terpenes), which have antioxidant power.

Papaya

This tropical pear-shaped fruit is quite large, growing up to 20 inches in length and 12 inches in diameter. The sweet flesh is mainly orange with touches of pink and amber. It exudes a strange almost cheese-like scent that some find appetizing and others find about as appealing as a pair of smelly socks. The odor does, however, dissipate when the fruit is blended with other ingredients.

Papaya is perhaps best known as an aid to digestion. It contains a particular enzyme (papain) that helps to digest protein and may also help ease some disorders related to incomplete digestion. It is itself easily digested and high in fiber, which further enhances its digestive properties. Papaya is a rich source of the antioxidants beta-carotene and vitamin C, and a good source of vitamin A and many of the B-group vitamins. It also provides moderate amounts of potassium, calcium, and iron. Interestingly, papaya seeds (which are edible but have a bitter taste) have long been used in folk medicine for their purported anti-inflammatory, antiparasitic, and analgesic properties, but these are yet to be scientifically proven.

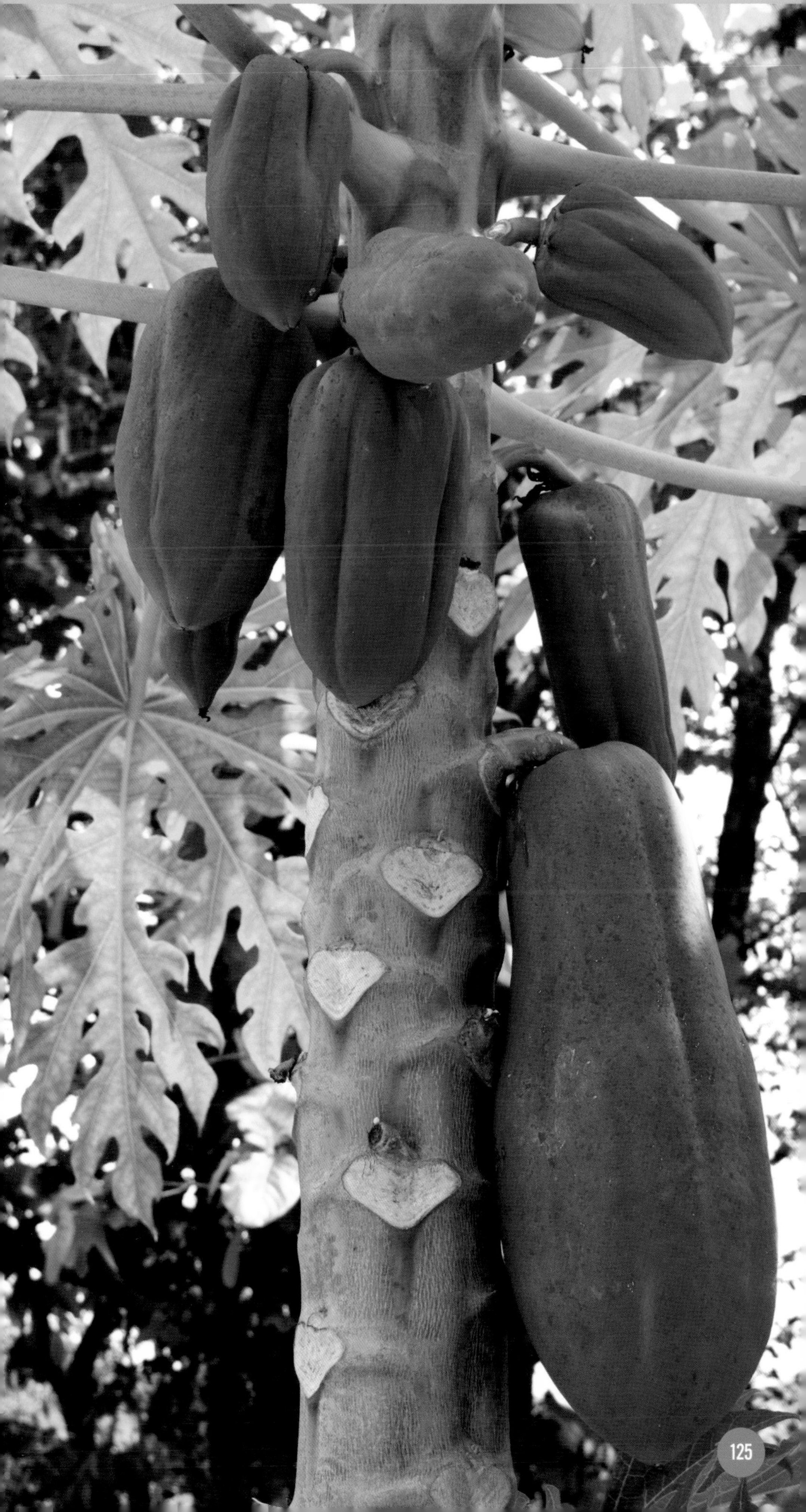

Peach

Delectable, health-promoting peaches have a sweet, juicy flesh that hosts a spectacular array of nutrients. Despite their sweetness, peaches are low in calories (less than 12 calories per ounce). Very ripe peaches can also be pulped and blended with water (or coconut water) to produce a delicious, nutritious nectar that is perfect for fruit smoothies, either on its own or blended with other fruits like grapes, cherries, and plums. Peaches are high in antioxidants, including vitamins A and C, beta-carotene, and lutein. It is widely believed that foods high in antioxidants may reduce the risk of cancer and degenerative diseases such as Alzheimer's disease, as well as assist in the treatment and prevention of other disorders. Peaches, especially the yellow variety, also contain useful amounts of minerals like potassium, considered helpful in the treatment of high blood pressure, as well as iron and manganese.

Pear

Close cousins of the apple, pears have a high water and fiber content and are very low-calorie, providing around 100 calories. They come in a wide range of varieties that, in broad terms, fall into two categories: the more firm and crisp Asian pears, and the European pears that soften as they ripen and therefore have traditionally been favored for juicing. Both Asian and European pears are suitable for smoothies, adding a pleasant, light, sweet taste. They are a good source of potassium and the antioxidant vitamin C, and also have modest levels of other nutrients, including beta-carotene and other antioxidants. Pears are very high in dietary fiber as well as sorbitol, which together provide laxative benefits. Pears are known as being one of the least allergenic of fruits and are therefore often recommended for inclusion in low-allergen diets.

Pea

See "Legumes" on page 111.

Pepper

There are several varieties of chili peppers, ranging from the large bell peppers ("capsicum") to the hot spicy cayenne pepper, which most people can tolerate only in small doses on account of its intense heat. Other varieties include jalapenos and pimentos. They are all fruits of the capsicum plant.

Bell peppers are crunchy and quite sweet to the taste, yet low in calories (1 ounce yields less than 10 calories). Like all peppers, they contain the chemical capsaicin. Preliminary research suggests that capsaicin might offer, among other benefits, antibacterial and anti-carcinogenic properties, and might assist in lowering LDL cholesterol. Bell peppers are a rich source of the antioxidants vitamin C, beta-carotene, and lutein. They are a good source of vitamin A, some B-group vitamins, and several minerals, in particular iron, manganese, magnesium, and potassium.

Cayenne peppers pack a punch in any savory smoothie. They contain high concentrations of nutrients, but can be consumed only in very small quantities due to their hot flavor. A high level of capsaicin is responsible for this heat, but also imbues these peppers with pain-relieving capabilities. It is thought that, when ingested, capsaicin is able to interrupt the transmission of pain messages to the brain, thereby diverting or otherwise reducing the pain experience. Cayenne peppers are a rich source of vitamin C and beta-carotene as well as other antioxidants. They are a good source of B-group vitamins and also contain various minerals.

Pineapple

The exotic appearance of tropical fruit has strong associations with celebrations and beachside holidays in the sun—and these alone are capable of conjuring up happy thoughts that in turn can be beneficial to health. Holidays and celebrations aside, the pineapple is in fact a compound fruit, meaning that it is not one but rather a number of smaller fruits fused together around the very fibrous core. Pineapple is an excellent source of vitamin C, and also contains modest quantities of a wide range of other nutrients. Of particular interest is the fact that it contains bromelain, an enzyme that breaks down protein and aids digestion. Bromelain also has anti-inflammatory, anti-clotting, and anti-cancer properties. While the pineapple core is less sweet than the flesh and so fibrous that it can be impossible to eat (unless pureed), it does contain bromelain and also offers digestive benefits. It is therefore worth including at least some of the core in smoothie blends.

Plum

This fleshy and succulent fruit is perhaps best known for aiding digestion. Most plums are a dark bluish-red color, and in their dried form they are known as prunes, long used to relieve constipation. Sorbitol, a sugar alcohol in plums, combined with a high soluble fiber content, is largely responsible for the fruit's gentle laxative effect. Plums and prunes are a good source of antioxidant vitamins C and A and also contain lutein and beta-carotene. They are an excellent source of potassium. Eating prunes on a regular basis may also be beneficial for bone health.

Pomegranate

This ancient and exotic fruit is hailed as a heart protector. Pomegranate seeds (arils) are rich in polyphenols, a powerful group of antioxidants that may offer significant health benefits, particularly relating to cardiovascular and prostate health. Research has shown that drinking a daily glass of pomegranate juice (made by blending the fruit's seeds) can reduce the risk of cardio-vascular disease by helping to clear clogged arteries. It may even reverse the progression of the disease. This pomegranate potion also has strong anti-inflammatory effects that result in improved blood flow and delayed oxidation of LDL cholesterol in patients with heart disease and arthritis. Pomegranates are a nutrition powerhouse and a good source of Vitamin C, potassium, B-group vitamins such as folate, vitamin K, and dietary fiber.

One of the best ways to remove the seeds from a pomegranate is to cut it in half and hit the backs with the side of a wooden spoon over a bowl.

Prune

See "Plum" on page 134.

Raspberry

Pretty and fragrant, raspberries have
an interesting structure. Each berry
is a collection of small drupes or
drupelets (small stone fruits), gathered
around a hollow center. Each drupelet has its
own tiny seed surrounded by the berry pulp.

Raspberries are a pinkish-red color, and
while mostly sweet, some varieties are
more tart or sour. They are low in calories,
high in fiber, and high in antioxidants,
including tannin and anthocyanin (which gives
them their color). While research is continuing,
scientific studies indicate that these antioxidants
may play an important role in fighting cancer, aging,
and various inflammatory and degenerative
diseases.

For such a little fruit, raspberries are
packed with nutrients, including particularly high
levels of vitamin C (also an antioxidant) and the
mineral manganese. They also contain potassium,
magnesium, iron, zinc, some B-group vitamins,
and vitamins E and K.

Raspberries are ideal for freezing, and can
then be used in place of ice cubes when making
smoothies.

Spices

Spices have long been used to preserve and enhance the flavor of food, as well as used in folk medicine. Some have a sweetening effect, others add heat, and still others complement certain flavors beautifully. While spices can be nutrient-dense, only tiny amounts are used, so they can only contribute to the recommended daily intake of certain nutrients rather than act as a sole source. Here are a few of the spices that work well in smoothies:

Cinnamon sticks

Cinnamon is a sweet, warm spice from the bark of the cinnamon tree. It has three essential oils, one of which (cinnamaldehyde) is thought to possess anti-inflammatory properties. The oils can also help stop the growth of bacteria and have antimicrobial properties. Some clinical trials have shown that a type of cinnamon, cinnamon cassia, can reduce spikes in blood sugar after eating and may have implications for the management of type-2 diabetes.

Cloves have long been used in folk medicine for their antiseptic and analgesic effects, but research to validate these claims is limited. Nonetheless, many attest to the seemingly numbing effect of cloves or clove oil, especially in relation to dental pain. Cloves have a warm, spicy flavor.

Cloves

Nutmeg is the seed of the nutmeg tree. Traditionally, it has been used in folk medicine for anxiety, insomnia, indigestion, and a host of other ailments, but these therapeutic benefits are as yet unproven. Nutmeg in large doses can have potentially dangerous side effects. Its main benefit is as a flavor enhancer due to its warm, sweet, spicy flavor.

Nutmeg

Turmeric is a richly colored, hot spice used in curries and some mustards, and it adds a kick to any savory smoothie. Turmeric contains an active compound called curcumin, which may be helpful in treating arthritic ailments. Turmeric is undergoing research for its possible role in the treatment and prevention of cancers, particularly of the gastro-intestinal tract, as well as Alzheimer's disease and various other disorders.

Ground turmeric

Spinach

One of the great leafy greens,
spinach is very low in calories,
high in fiber, and exceptionally
high in a spectacular array of
vitamins, minerals, and other
nutrients. It is well known for its high
iron content, but is also a rich source of
vitamins A and C, lutein, beta-carotene,
and zeaxanthin. These antioxidants are known
for their ability to neutralize free radicals. This
benefits heart, brain, and eye health, and lowers the
risk of degenerative diseases such as Alzheimer's.
Spinach is also high in vitamin K and includes
several B-group vitamins. Potassium, manganese,
magnesium, copper, and zinc are also found in its
leaves. Fresh, young spinach leaves are best in
smoothies. The leaves, while high in fiber, are also
soft, and have a delicate flavor.

Strawberry

This popular little berry is pinkish-red in color and boasts the unusual feature of having seeds outside rather than inside its flesh. This gives it a peculiar, yet attractive, tailored appearance. The flavor is sweet but slightly tart, and combines very well in smoothies with other berries and fruits. Strawberries are packed with vitamin C and other antioxidants, including anthocyanins (the pigment that is responsible for their color), ellagic acid, vitamins A and E, beta-carotene, lutein, and zeaxanthin.

The antioxidants in strawberries are thought to contribute to the fight against cancer, as well as degenerative and inflammatory diseases. Additionally, strawberries contain various minerals, including manganese, iron, potassium, and magnesium. Like all berries, they are highly perishable, but if frozen when fresh, they can be added to smoothies later in the form of ice blocks without any compromise to their nutritional value.

Swiss Chard

Swiss chard is up there with spinach as one of the great green leafers that offers a host of health benefits. It's low in calories; high in fiber; high in antioxidants, including vitamins C and A, beta-carotene, and lutein; high in many B-group vitamins; and a good source of iron, magnesium, manganese, copper, and potassium. It is no surprise that Swiss chard is touted as one of the most health-giving vegetables. A small handful in a smoothie blended together with other greens or perhaps some sweeter fruits and berries packs a nutritional punch into the day.

Rainbow Swiss chard is a variety of Swiss chard that features brightly-colored stems.

Rainbow Swiss chard

Tomato

Often thought to be a vegetable, the tomato is actually a fruit that boasts an enormous number of health-promoting properties. First and foremost, tomatoes are high in lycopene, a powerful antioxidant. Other antioxidants found in tomatoes include beta-carotene, zeaxanthin, and vitamins C and A. These power molecules neutralize free radicals in the body and help prevent certain cancers and other diseases. Tomatoes are also rich in potassium and have average amounts of several other vitamins and minerals. Tomatoes are flavorful and juicy, and they blend well in smoothies with other fruits and vegetables, particularly celery and peppers. Due to their high water content, tomatoes are an ideal base for a number of smoothies—but they also work exceptionally well as almost the only ingredient, perhaps accompanied by a few healthy herbs and spices.

Watermelon

See "Melons" on page 120.

Additional Ingredients

Protein Supplements

These can be broadly classified into two groups: those that provide protein only, and those that provide both protein and carbohydrates. Both types often include additional ergogenic (performance-boosting) ingredients, such as vitamins, minerals, creatine, specific amino acids, and proposed fat metabolizers.

Protein-only supplements are typically 90 percent protein by weight, while those with added carbohydrates vary, with the protein content as little as 10 percent up to 50 percent. Protein that contains essential amino acids in a proportion similar to that required by humans is said to have a high biological value (HBV). There is a wide range of protein supplements available. Use only the amount specified by the manufacturer, and keep in mind that it is generally necessary to increase water intake when ingesting these.

Whey Protein: This is a HBV protein that is rapidly digested, and is comprised of approximately 20 percent dairy protein. Whey is rich in branched-chain amino acids, especially leucine, the amino acid primarily responsible for stimulating protein synthesis. Recent evidence suggests that whey protein may offer greater satiety than other whole proteins, alluding to a potential role in weight loss as well as weight gain. There are three main forms of whey protein:

- Whey protein concentrate (WPC): Derived from the first filtering step in the production of whey protein isolate, it is typically 70 to 80 percent protein by weight with small amounts of lactose (milk sugar) and fat. It is cheaper than whey protein isolate.

- Whey protein isolate (WPI): Further filtration of WPC produces this powder that is

Whey protein powder

approximately 90 percent protein by weight, with negligible amounts of carbohydrates (lactose) and fat.

- Whey protein hydrolysate (WPH): This is derived from either WPC or WPI and supposedly assists in even more rapid digestion and absorption, with a greater insulin response. Evidence to date is preliminary and conflicting. The process of hydrolysis used to produce the powder is more expensive and produces a bitter taste.

Casein or Calcium Caseinate: This HBV protein makes up about 80 percent of the protein in milk. Casein forms clots in the stomach, slowing digestion and the delivery of amino acids to the body. Casein hydrolysates are also available, resulting in a more rapidly digested and absorbed protein.

Soy Protein: This HBV protein is rapidly digested. As with whey, it is available as both a soy concentrate and a soy isolate, and is often used in supplements made up of protein from mixed sources because it is cheaper than whey. There is evidence to suggest that women with existing or previous breast cancer should be cautious in consuming large quantities of soy foods. The Cancer Council does not recommend or support the use of supplements such as soy protein.

Spirulina is blue-green algae found in salt water and is promoted as a source of dietary protein, vitamin A, B-vitamins (especially B12), and iron. Similar products have been around for a long time and are said to be beneficial for many conditions, ranging from

Spirulina powder

hay fever to the prevention of precancerous growths in the mouth. So far, however, there isn't enough evidence to determine whether or not they are effective. Other claims say spirulina is a good appetite suppressant and boosts energy levels.

Dairy and Dairy Alternatives

Dairy products are highly nutritious. Cow's milk, for example, is regarded as a complete food because it contains all the nutrients necessary to sustain life. Most of the recipes in this book that use milk suggest milk alternatives, such as almond milk, because they blend well in smoothies without making them too heavy, they are suitable for people who are lactose-intolerant, and they are generally lower in calories. Low-fat dairy milk can, however, be used instead. Any of the other types of milk alternatives, including oat milk and soy milk, can also be used, but whenever using a substitute be sure to check the nutrition panel on the packaging. Choose fortified milk substitutes that are high in calcium and other nutrients and relatively low in calories—and choose low-fat varieties. Many coconut milks are unfortunately very high in fat, so coconut water is often a healthier option.

Almond milk is made from ground almonds and, perhaps, a sweetener. It is rich in vitamin E but has less protein and calcium than regular cow's milk.

Coconut milk has as a similar "mouth feel" to dairy milk and a distinct coconut flavor. It is high in saturated fat and very low in protein and

calcium compared with dairy milk. But it is suitable for vegans if they are able to obtain their calcium from other sources.

Oat milk is made from ground oats and water. It contains some dietary fiber and various vitamins and minerals. It is low in calcium, although commercial varieties are often fortified with calcium.

Yogurt and other fermented foods are an important part of the diet. Yogurts with probiotics (healthy bacteria) help to keep our gut flora in balance and our digestive and immune systems functioning well. Yogurt is also an excellent source of high-quality protein, calcium, B-group vitamins, and all the other nutrients found in dairy milk. People with lactose intolerance may find it easier to tolerate yogurt than milk because the bacteria partly digest the lactose. Coconut yogurt is similar nutritionally to coconut milk. It is very high in saturated fat and very low in protein. It has negligible calcium and sugar. Many of the commercial coconut yogurts are sweetened with xylitol (see page 155).

Grains

Oats are high in energy-giving carbohydrates and an excellent source of beta-glucan soluble fiber, which reduces cholesterol reabsorption. Oats are low GI so they help maintain blood glucose control and are very satisfying.

Quinoa is an ancient pseudo-grain, part seed and part grain, originating from South America. It has been touted as a supergrain. Nutritionally, it is very high in protein and dietary fiber. It is also rich in an array of important minerals like iron, magnesium, and zinc. As it is gluten-free, it makes an excellent high-fiber choice for people with celiac disease or gluten intolerance. It needs to be pre-cooked and chilled for use in smoothies.

Wheat germ is a rich source of vitamin E and a good source of many other vitamins, especially the B-group. It contains the minerals selenium, iron, and zinc and is a good plant source of omega-3 fats, which have an anti-inflammatory role in the body.

Sweeteners

Ideally, all smoothies can be enjoyed without sweetener, but sometimes a little sweetening makes them more palatable, especially to children. Try to reduce the amount used over time as palettes adjust to the natural flavors. If sweeteners are used, choose natural ones, such as stevia or monk fruit. Other sweeteners like honey and maple syrup are also suitable if used only occasionally and in moderation, as they are high in calories.

Agave syrup, from the agave plant, is sweeter than honey and lower in calories, but it has a very high fructose content.

Fructose is a simple sugar found naturally in most fruit and also in honey. It has the same calorie value as table sugar and a low GI.

High-fructose corn syrup is not the same as fructose. It is a mixture of glucose and fructose and has a high GI. High-fructose corn syrup has been added to many foods in the United States as a sweetener and is considered to be a major contributor to the obesity epidemic.

Honey is considered to be more natural than cane sugar, but it is still a sugar—a combination of glucose, fructose, and water. It is nonetheless an ideal natural sweetener. It has a delicious sweet and rich flavor, making it an ideal sweetener in smoothies. Honey also contains small amounts of some B vitamins and other nutrients. It has a long history in folk medicine and beauty treatments— uses include the treatment of sore throats and coughs, high blood pressure, constipation, and wounds; face masks; and hair treatments. It also appears to have a calming effect, which some claim is powerful when combined with other

ingredients like chamomile. Many also believe that honey may have antibacterial and anti-inflammatory properties, and it has long been used in holistic medicine for these purposes. However, these claims are yet to be proven conclusively. As a word of caution, honey should not be given to children under the age of one year because of the small chance that it may contain botulism.

Maple syrup is the concentrated sap from the maple tree. It has some useful nutrients, but the quantities are very small and hence the benefits limited. The syrup is composed almost entirely of sugar, but it is nonetheless a natural sweetener and more nutritious than refined sugars.

Monk fruit comes from a Chinese plant and has no calories. The active ingredient is an intensely sweet glucose molecule (200 to 400 times sweeter than table sugar) that is blended with other ingredients.

Monk fruit

Stevia is extracted from the leaves of the stevia plant. It is 250 to 300 times sweeter than sugar, and some find it leaves a bitter aftertaste. A teaspoon is equal to one cup of table sugar.

Sucrose, otherwise known as table sugar, is half fructose and half glucose. Just one teaspoon has 16 calories.

Xylitol is a natural carbohydrate found in fibrous fruit and vegetables. It has 40 percent fewer calories than table sugar. However, excessive amounts can have a laxative effect, and some people find it difficult to tolerate.

Seeds

Seeds are very nutritious and packed full of the antioxidant vitamin E, fiber, healthy fats, B-group vitamins, calcium, magnesium, copper, iron, and zinc. They also add a lot of flavor to food (especially if roasted).

Chia, an ancient Aztec grain, rivals flaxseed as a plant source of omega-3s. Chia seeds are very high in soluble dietary fiber, which forms a viscous gel that lowers the blood glucose response and increases satiety, helping us feel fuller for longer.

Chia seeds

Flaxseed (also known as linseed) is a good plant source of omega-3s called alpha-linolenic acid (ALA). Flaxseed also contains lignans, a group of phytoestrogens that help to alleviate hot flashes during menopause. Of all seeds, they have one of the highest concentrations of lignans.

Hemp seeds are another good source of omega-3 fats and fiber. They also contain gamma-linolenic acid (GLA), which has anti-inflammatory properties and helps with conditions such as rheumatoid arthritis, allergies, and eczema. Containing all essential amino acids, hemp seeds are a good quality protein for vegans. Hemp seeds contain vitamins E, C, and the B-group, as well as iron and magnesium.

Pumpkin seeds (pepitas) are a good source of protein and fiber. Rich in magnesium, iron, zinc, and copper, they are also high in essential fatty acids and contain twice as much unsaturated fats as saturated fats. They are a good source of the antioxidant vitamin E and contain tryptophan, which the body converts to the mood-enhancer serotonin. This may be of benefit in the treatment of anxiety disorders.

Pumpkin seeds

Sesame seeds are an excellent plant source of protein and calcium. They have a mix of monounsaturated and polyunsaturated fats, and are highest of all seeds in plant sterols, which help lower cholesterol absorption.

Sunflower seeds are a rich source of omega-6s and a good source of vitamin E, as well as minerals like magnesium, copper, and selenium. Sunflower seeds contain phytosterols, compounds found in plants that appear to reduce cholesterol levels and strengthen immune function.

Nuts

Nuts have well and truly made a healthy comeback with compelling research showing that regular nut nibblers can dramatically reduce their risk of heart disease. Nuts include healthy fats, dietary fiber, arginine, plant sterols, and range of vitamins and minerals known to be important for heart health (including folate, magnesium, potassium, zinc, copper, and vitamin E).

Each tree nut has its own unique nutrient makeup, and there's new research emerging for every arm of the family tree. All nuts contain vitamin E, a fat-soluble vitamin and potent antioxidant that helps protect tissues from damage. Vitamin E is thought to play a role in heart health by protecting LDL (bad) cholesterol from attaching to and blocking blood vessel walls. An average serving (1 ounce) of mixed nuts provides about 20 percent of the recommended dietary intake (RDI) of vitamin E.

Almonds are one of the richest nut sources of vitamin E—a small handful provides as much as 85 percent of the RDI. Be sure to eat almonds with their brown skins, as the anti-oxidant properties are found in the skin.

Brazil nuts are so-named because they are the seeds of an enormous tree found in the Amazon rain forest. They are an excellent

Brazil nuts

source of selenium, a vital mineral and antioxidant that may help prevent tissue damage. Eating Brazil nuts can help boost your daily intake of selenium, with just two Brazil nuts providing your entire recommended dietary intake of selenium.

Chestnuts are a little different from other tree nuts in their makeup. They contain very little fat and protein and are made up predominantly of carbohydrates and water, which makes them lower in calories than other nuts are. A one-ounce serving has approximately 60 calories compared with over 178 calories in the same size serving of almonds.

Hazelnuts are a great source of dietary fiber, particularly the outer skin, or testa, which protects bowel health and can help lower cholesterol levels. Dietary fiber together with the protein content in nuts helps with feeling full after a meal, also known as satiety. With the highest dietary fiber score of over 10 percent fiber content, a small handful of hazelnuts makes a great snack and will help you feel fuller for longer.

Macadamias are brimming with healthy monounsaturated fats and have been found to lower blood cholesterol. They also contain plant sterols similar to those found in the new-age, cholesterol-lowering margarines (the ones that don't have trans fat). These plant sterols have compounds that are thought to contribute to the cholesterol-lowering effect of nuts.

Pistachios, with their unique green color, are considered a luxury and are often used only as a prized garnish in traditional Middle Eastern recipes. They are rich in protein. About 60 pistachios make up an average nut serving.

Walnuts are also a rich source of alpha-linolenic acid (ALA, a plant-based omega-3 fat). Research has shown that ALA from walnuts can reduce inflammation, similar to the way omega-3 fats from fish do.

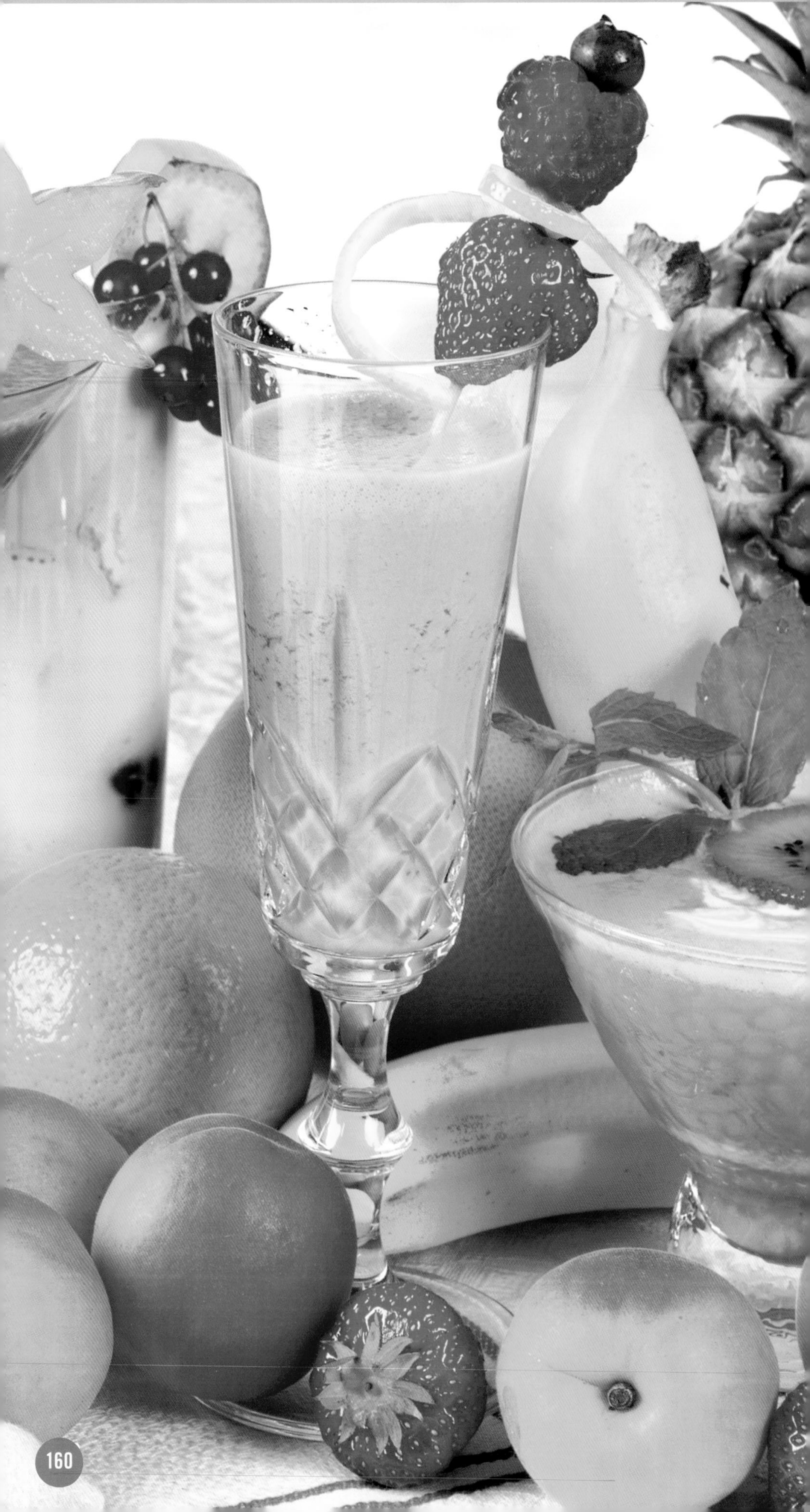

TOP 10 SMOOTHIE TIPS

1. Smoothie Too Thick? Just Add Water

Most smoothies will blend into a thick yet drinkable consistency, but if your smoothie is too thick just add some extra water. The consistency will depend not just on how much liquid you have added, but also on the amount of water in other ingredients—and if there are any that will soak up fluids the way grains and fiber supplements do.

2. Smoothie Too Thin? Add Some Extras

If you need to thicken up a smoothie, add some fibrous ingredients such as apple, banana, mango, avocado, or even oats or flaxseed. Don't be afraid to make adjustments as you go. Remember that the color and texture of your smoothies will vary each time, depending on natural variations in the ingredients and the amount of liquid added.

3. Get the Most from Your Smoothie

To reap the most benefit from your smoothie, ensure that the main ingredients are fresh fruit and/or vegetables and water (or ice).

4. Try Frozen Fruit

Mix in some frozen fruit and vegetables instead of ice blocks or if certain fresh ingredients are not available—but always be sure the main ingredients are fresh fruit and vegetables. Be aware, too, that while the quantities of fruit and vegetables in smoothies can more-or-less be varied according to personal taste, the same does not apply to other ingredients like protein supplements, milk and milk alternatives, nuts and seeds, and grains (see pages 150–58).

5. Wash the Ingredients

Always wash vegetables and fruit before using.

6. If Fiber is Needed . . .

Seeds, such as chia and flaxseed (linseed), are particularly good for easing constipation and other such issues. Fiber supplements are not generally needed in smoothies but, if they are used, they should be of the soluble type. Never use more than the quantities suggested on their packaging, and use them only in conjunction with lots of extra water.

7. Make Your Own Milk Alternative

Additional liquids can be used, such as nut milks, oat milk, and coconut milk. In most cases, you can make these yourself—home-made almond milk, for example, is both delicious and nutritious. Be sure to use treated almonds (untreated raw almonds are toxic), and use a proven recipe that also gives a nutritional breakdown. If you are buying these milks, choose quality ones and read the nutritional labels. Be mindful of fat and sugar content, and look for milks that are fortified with calcium and vitamins such as B12. Dairy milk is another option, but many people find nut and cereal milks such as oat milk to be more compatible with green smoothies than dairy milk is.

8. Give Your Smoothie a Yogurt Boost

Yogurt added to smoothies can boost their nutritional value, improve digestion, and offer a huge range of benefits specific to yogurt (and other fermented foods). This is mainly due to the good bacteria yogurt

contains. Yogurt produced from dairy sources is fine, and soy and coconut yogurts can be ideal for vegans. Generally, low-fat yogurts are better than high fat. Always choose natural yogurt over sweetened or flavored varieties, and pick high-quality brands. Yogurt can add significantly to the calorie count of a smoothie, so only a tablespoon or two is plenty (see also page 153).

9.   Add Some Seeds, Grains and Nuts

Grains can be added to your smoothie—oats work particularly well, giving a smooth richness when blended with water. Quinoa is also very nutritious and has a high protein content (see page 153).

Small amounts of seeds and nuts also work well, either in the smoothie itself or ground (if required) and sprinkled on top—but "small" is important. Nuts and seeds are high in calories. Also, it is thought that not all of their nutrients are available to the human body when consumed in the unground form because they are enclosed in an indigestible part of the nut or seed and pass through the system. But when nuts and seeds are ground, as occurs when making a smoothie, those indigestible parts (and their calories) become partially digestible.

Keep in mind that many nuts, seeds, and their oils have potent ingredients. One example is the Brazil nut. Although wonderfully nutritious, it also contains very high amounts of selenium, which has a number of health benefits but can be harmful if taken in high amounts. An excess can cause stomach upsets, irritability, and tiredness, among other things. Too much consumed over too long a period has the potential to cause some very serious health disorders. Yet few people realize how little is enough, and how quickly the threshold can be crossed. Adults can generally tolerate up to 400 mg per day, yet just half an ounce—about three nuts—contains this much! Only a maximum of three nuts can be consumed per day, and less if other foods containing selenium are also eaten. The quantities that can be tolerated by children are, of course, lower.

Warning! "More" is not always better!

10. Tempt a Fussy Palate with Herbs, Spices, and Vanilla

Sweeteners can be added, but are not generally necessary (see pages 154–55). A healthier option is to sweeten smoothies naturally through the use of fruit. Some herbs, such as mint, can also have a sweetening effect without significant calories and without causing dental problems, as do small amounts of cinnamon or vanilla.

Taking Care with Nuts and Seeds

Some nuts and seeds are not suitable for human consumption and should not be added to smoothies. One example is the seeds of stone fruits—including peaches, mangoes, nectarines, cherries, and avocados— because they contain a substance (amygdalin) that the body converts to cyanide. Apple and pear seeds also contain amygdalin, although given their small size they present less risk than that of the larger pits.

Apart from the cyanide issue, some pits, when ground into a smoothie, will add a bitter flavor. More importantly, grinding may release toxins that would otherwise pass unnoticed through the system, safely secured within the seed's hard, indigestible shell.

Importantly, the seeds of the guava and cactus pear should never be added to smoothies—when ground, they can effectively be the same as ground glass and hence can scratch, cut, and otherwise damage the digestive tract.

Almonds also pose particular problems, and should not be consumed raw; even almonds sold as "raw" have been treated in some way to remove toxic components.

With all this in mind, it is recommended that when making smoothies, (a) all pits and seeds should be removed except for the tiny edible ones found in such fruits as berries, passion fruit, kiwifruit, and tomatoes, as well as arils found in pomegranates; (b) the amount of edible nuts and seeds added to smoothies should be limited; (c) if including nuts and seeds, add only those known to be edible when ground—don't be adventurous in this area; (d) if using almonds, use properly prepared almond milk rather than almonds; and (e) be aware of the potential for allergic reactions to certain nuts or peanuts.

RECIPES

The following pages include 100 smoothie recipes, all of which provide a number of benefits. They have been broadly grouped into eight categories, just to give some focus, but this should not limit them. For example, the smoothies in the "Beauty Box" category might be of particular interest to those looking for ways to improve their skin, but that is not all that those smoothies do! They all offer a cross-range of benefits. So, dip in, experiment, and have fun enjoying these smooth little health boosters.

All the recipes are intended as a launch pad for your own ideas; smoothies are super easy to make, and once you have made a few you will quickly start to come up with your own ideas, experimenting with different ingredients and flavor combinations. You'll also start to experience their goodness for yourself, and learn more about how your own body responds to certain ingredients. And soon you will develop your own list of favorites.

Happy Days

A plan to balance mood and promote feelings of well-being

Food has a major effect on how we think, and also on our mood. Glucose is the food of the brain, and glucose comes from food. Without glucose, our brains can't function at all, and if it is depleted we will become fuzzy-headed and unable to think clearly.

Glucose is so important for our brain function, and indeed our lives, that if there is not enough glucose from carbohydrates, our bodies will first start accessing fat stores and then move on to the protein in our body in order to feed the brain. In effect, in extreme situations, our bodies will begin consuming themselves to power the brain.

Vitamins, minerals, and phytochemicals (see pages 25–39) are also vital for our emotional well-being. When there are deficiencies, not only are our bodies physically compromised—so are our moods. The effects may range from irritability, impatience, and stress all the way to anxiety and depression, among other things.

While deficiencies can adversely affect mood, higher quantities of some foods appear to have the ability to lift mood. This is an exciting area of ongoing research; while some foods have been proven to be beneficial to mood, the knowledge about others is still sketchy but appears positive.

Blood Sugar Levels

Low blood sugar (glucose) levels in the blood has an impact on mood and health. Serious conditions such as "true" hypoglycemia and diabetes are directly linked to blood sugar, but even in healthy people, temporary drops in blood sugar are very likely to cause irritability, impatience, tiredness, frustration, anger, and other negative emotions, along with some physical symptoms and fuzzy-headedness. There is also a type of

hypoglycemia known as "reactive" or "rebound" (rather than "true") hypoglycemia, which is its opposite; it is caused when the blood sugar level rises too quickly after eating, and can also result in unpleasant symptoms, including anxiety, poor concentration, and irritability, among other things. There is no one-size-fits-all remedy to unpleasant moods and mood swings, but a combination of lifestyle approaches and good eating habits will help achieve more balanced moods and a feeling of well-being. It is clear, for example, that blood sugar levels need to be kept stable, and in terms of diet the low-GI (low glycemic index) has proven to be very effective in this area.

In a low-GI diet, high-GI carbohydrates are avoided in favor of low-GI carbohydrates, which release glucose gradually and steadily into the bloodstream instead of in one "sugar hit" (see also pages 36–37). The mineral chromium also helps to manage blood sugar levels.

Mood-Boosting Nutrients

Furthermore, although they are the subject of continued research and much debate, eleven key nutrients have been identified as helping to boost mood and also overcome depression. They are: calcium, chromium, folate, iron, magnesium, omega-3 fats, vitamin B6, vitamin B12, vitamin D, zinc, and selenium. Generally, we are not able to source much, if any, vitamin D through food sources, nor vitamin B12 through plant sources alone, but the remaining nutrients are easily found in plants. For vitamin D, the main source is sunshine. Vitamin B12 is found in animal and dairy foods; yogurt is a good source that works well in smoothies (see also page 153), but always use a high-quality, no-sugar plain yogurt, and check the label on the packaging for its nutritional value.

Tryptophan

Another very important factor in mood balance is the amino acid tryptophan, which the body converts into serotonin. Serotonin is known as the "feel good" substance in the body, for it promotes calm and serenity as well as helps with sleep (which also improves mood!). Spinach, watercress, mint, and parsley are good sources, along with lots of other leafy green vegetables.

There is a wealth of information about "feel good" diets, some of it conflicting and some of it still in the early stages of research. But, it would seem that smoothies containing some or all of the nutrients mentioned will in some way benefit mood, and are nonetheless beneficial to health in a number of other ways. This means lots of leafy greens, bananas, mangoes, berries, avocados, flaxseed, and cinnamon in our smoothies, along with other nutritious ingredients. As always, it pays to experiment, and to monitor our own responses over time. On the following pages are a few ideas to get you started.

Mango Tango

1 peeled banana
a handful of baby spinach leaves
1 peeled, pitted, and diced mango
½ cup water
2 tbsp yogurt
3–4 ice cubes
mint for garnish (optional)

This luscious smoothie is both sweet and satisfying. Add a little ginger if you want a bit more kick.

Feel-good nutrients: chromium, magnesium, vitamin B6, vitamin B12, calcium, iron, folate

Easy As ABC

½ peeled and pitted avocado
1 peeled banana
2 tbsp cacao
½ cup water
3–4 ice cubes
stevia or other sweetener (to taste)

The avocado adds a creamy richness that tastes almost decadent and blends divinely with the cacao. The water works nicely, but for an indulgent touch, substitute a low-fat coconut milk.

Feel-good nutrients: chromium, magnesium, vitamin B6, calcium, iron, folate

Facing page: Mango Tango
Top: Easy As ABC

Bananaberry Bonanza

1 peeled banana
1 cup mixed berries
a small handful of baby spinach leaves
½ cup water
3–4 ice cubes
mint for garnish (optional)

No one can resist the pretty pinks and reds of berries and their sweet, sometimes slightly tart, taste. The banana in this smoothie helps bind all the ingredients together for a rich, smooth finish.

Feel-good nutrients: chromium, magnesium, vitamin B6, calcium, iron, omega-3 fats, folate

3-B-Baby

1 cup blueberries
1 peeled banana
½ cup broccoli
½ cup water
3–4 ice cubes
stevia or other sweetener (to taste)

More berries! More bananas! And now some broccoli, too!

Feel-good nutrients: zinc, chromium, magnesium, vitamin B6, calcium, iron, folate

Facing page: 3-B-Baby
Top: Bananaberry Bonanza

Mangoberrylicious

1 cup strawberries

1 peeled and pitted mango

½ cup broccoli

½ cup water

3–4 ice cubes

mint for garnish (optional)

Another sweet, delicious smoothie bursting with mood-boosting nutrients. This one also works very well with high-quality almond or coconut milk in place of water.

Feel-good nutrients: chromium, folate

Beet, Beet, Beetin' the Blues

1 peeled beet

½ carrot

2 peeled and de-seeded oranges

1–2 thin slices of ginger

1 tbsp chia seeds

½ cup water

3–4 ice cubes

A tasty, tangy smoothie that helps keep the blues at bay.

Feel-good nutrients: calcium, zinc, folate, magnesium, vitamin B6

Facing page: Beet, Beet, Beetin' the Blues
Top: Mangoberrylicious

Open Sesame!

½ peeled banana

2 peeled and de-seeded oranges

2 tbsp sesame seeds

1 peeled and pitted mango

1 cup water

2–4 ice cubes

1 tsp grated nutmeg

Is this smoothie the gateway to good health and happiness? Maybe! Use good quality almond milk instead of water if you prefer.

Feel-good nutrients: chromium, magnesium, vitamin B, calcium, folate, zinc, omega-3s, iron, calcium

Kiwi-Kale-a-Cado

3 peeled kiwfruits

½ peeled and pitted avocado

1 generous handful of baby kale leaves

½ cup water

3–4 ice cubes

Kiwifruit is an odd-looking, fuzzy, almost egg-shaped fruit. The edible peel is rich in fiber and nutrients, so it can be used if desired. (One skin of the three is sufficient.)

Feel-good nutrients: folate, calcium, chromium, iron, omega-3s

Facing page: Kiwi-Kale-a-Cado
Top: Open Sesame!

Flax Attack

a small handful of baby spinach leaves

1 peeled and pitted mango

1 peeled banana

1 tbsp flaxseed

½ cup water

3–4 ice cubes

stevia or other sweetener (to taste)

It's not hard to get loads of fiber into your day if you throw a little flax into your smoothie. Almond milk can be used instead of water.

Feel-good nutrients: chromium, folate, omega-3 fats

Good Morning Kale!

1 small carrot

3 peeled and de-seeded oranges

1 generous handful of kale leaves

½ cup water

¼ tsp orange zest to garnish

Facing page: Good Morning Kale!
Top: Flax Attack (garnished with coconut, cacao powder, and mango)

The orange in this smoothie makes for a delightful and energetic start to the day, but the less-glamorous yet hard-working kale, together with the trusty carrot, underpin it with a truckload of extra nutrition.

Feel-good nutrients: calcium, zinc, folate, iron, omega-3s

Chocolate Wonderland

2 tbsp cacao powder or nibs

2 tbsp yogurt

1 cup mixed berries

½ cup coconut water or water

3–4 ice cubes

stevia or other sweetener

mint for garnish (optional)

This smoothie is so luscious that it's difficult to consume without little tweaks of guilt—which thankfully can be quickly banished!

Feel-good nutrients: iron, chromium, vitamin B12

Nutrition Bomb

1 peeled and de-seeded orange

½ peeled banana

a small handful of baby spinach leaves

1 peeled and pitted mango

1 tsp sesame seeds

1 Brazil nut

1 tbsp yogurt

½ cup water

½ cup ice cubes

This one's almost got it all—the only thing missing is vitamin D, so drink it in while soaking up the sun at a seaside location!

Feel-good nutrients: calcium, iron, chromium, folate, magnesium, omega-3s, vitamin B6, vitamin B12, zinc, selenium

Facing page: Chocolate Wonderland
Top: Nutrition Bomb

Fountain of Youth

A plan to minimize and counteract some of the effects of aging

Scientists can't yet promise eternal youth, but lots of nutrients found in food have been proven to help keep us looking and feeling young, with a spring in our step, and to keep our brain buzzing—or at least help us age well and get the most out of life through our senior years.

While all nutrients help us age well, in one way or another, the big contributors are the antioxidants and omega-3 fats, particularly for their various associations with brain health, cardiovascular and heart health, anti-inflammatory properties, and perhaps cancer prevention. Other nutrients that also warrant a mention here are the B-group vitamins, necessary for a range of things that become of increasing concern as we age, including energy, healthy skin and eyes, and healthy brain function; calcium, for its ability to help prevent osteoporosis as we age; and magnesium and vitamin K, also needed for brain health, among other things. A diet full of essential nutrients is needed throughout our lives—but we need even more of the "good stuff" as we age.

Antioxidants

Antioxidants, in broad terms, are molecules that stabilize "free radicals" (or "oxidants") inside the body. Free radicals are electronically charged molecules that react easily with and damage other molecules. Some vitamins and minerals have powerful antioxidant properties (particularly vitamins A, C, and E), selenium, zinc, and the phytonutrients that give fruits and vegetables their rich colors. These include, for example, beta-carotene and

anthocyanin. Antioxidants are said to help protect against and also treat certain cancers, help maintain good eyesight, and help prevent LDL ("bad" cholesterol) from being oxidized. LDL cholesterol is even more dangerous when oxidized because it increases the risk of narrowed, hardened arteries (a condition known as atherosclerosis) and hence the risk of heart attack or stroke.

Omega-3

Omega-3 fats have several benefits related to the management of aging. Most importantly, they support the heart and cardiovascular system. They are invaluable in helping to control cholesterol levels in the blood and preventing the buildup of plaque on artery walls, which leads to atherosclerosis. They assist in preventing clots from forming in the blood, another cause of heart attacks and stroke. They help counteract other potentially dangerous conditions such as irregular heartbeats and high levels of triglycerides (a fat found in the blood). Further, they also help in the treatment of high blood pressure because they make the arteries more elastic and therefore more able to handle the pressure.

Omega-3 fats are also needed to create three key fatty acids that our bodies need to function: ALA, EPA, and DHA. Perhaps surprisingly, 50 percent of the brain is fats, of which DHA is the most abundant. DHA has a particular role in the nerve-signal trans-missions that occur in the brain. Omega-3 fats, especially those with DHA, are essential for keeping the brain healthy, and particularly so as we age. There is a catch for those who derive most or all of their omega-3 fats from plant sources. Many plant sources of omega-3 fats also have significant quantities of omega-6 fats. These are similar to omega-3 fats but are sometimes described as "competitors" in part because omega-6 fats appear to inhibit the body's ability to convert omega-3 fats into the much-needed DHA. While omega-6

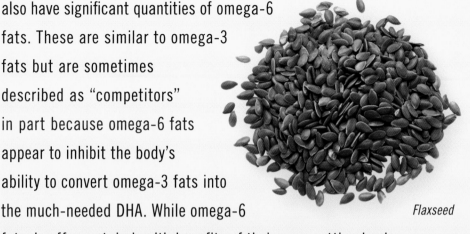

Flaxseed

fats do offer certain health benefits of their own, cutting back on omega-6 fats in favor of omega-3 fats is generally recommended. This is thought to be particularly important for those deriving their omega-3s from plant sources like nuts, rather than animal sources such as fish.

It follows that the best sources of plant-based omega-3 fats are those high in omega-3 but low in omega-6 (known as having the "lowest omega-6 to omega-3 ratio"). These include flaxseed, chia seeds, hemp, mustard oil, seaweed, mung beans, spinach, kale, blueberries, cloves, mangoes, papaya, and honeydew melon. Generous consumption of these is needed in order to get sufficient omega-3s and in turn reap the health benefits.

For those on strict vegan diets, getting enough omega-3s can be a challenge, and may warrant suitable dietary supplements. This is especially the case with older people. As well as supporting the heart, cardiovascular system, and brain, omega-3 fats also help prevent age-related macular degeneration.

B-Group Vitamins

These are essential for brain health, and one study found that three in particular—vitamins B6, B12, and folate—work together to help protect the brain from various conditions including Alzheimer's disease, and to improve brain function generally. B-group vitamins are also said to improve vascular function.

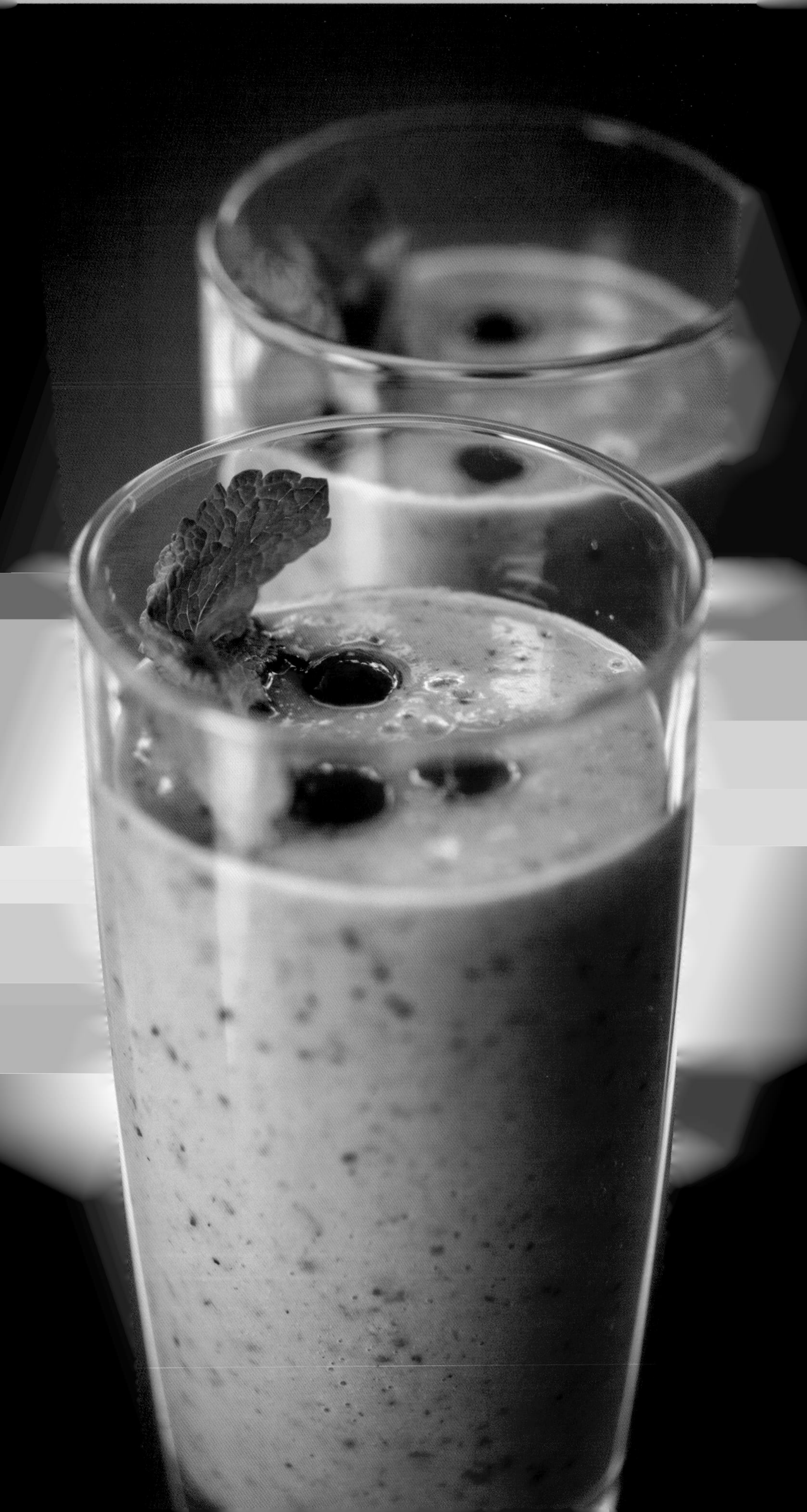

123–O.M.G.

½ peeled and de-seeded honeydew
melon
½ peeled and de-seeded papaya
¼ cup water
1 tbsp flaxseed
½ teaspoon ground cloves
3–4 ice cubes

Oh my gosh—it's omega-3!—and lots of it. Enjoy this smoothie on a regular basis to help keep your brain buzzing.

Biggest brain-boosters:
omega-3 fats

Brain Train

¼ cup blackberries
¼ cup strawberries
¼ cup raspberries
¼ cup blueberries
a small handful of baby spinach leaves
½ cup almond milk
3–4 ice cubes
stevia or other sweetener (to taste)

Facing page: Brain Train
Top: 123–O.M.G.

Berries are full of brain-boosting antioxidants, and the leafy greens such as spinach pack a punch in this area, too. They help in other ways as well—but first and foremost they are such an easy way to feed our minds!

Biggest brain-boosters: antioxidants

Hot Saucy Mama

3 tomatoes

½ bell pepper

½ de-seeded chili pepper

1 peeled cucumber

¼ peeled onion

1 clove garlic

small handful of parsley

¼ teaspoon turmeric, to taste

a splash or two of water

3–4 ice cubes

This is a variation of the Spanish chilled soup gazpacho and is a rich concoction of antioxidants, anti-inflammatories, and other nutrients. There's also sulfur-rich onion and garlic—so be sure to include plenty of parsley to keep the breath fresh!

Best anti-agers: antioxidants, anti-inflammatories, and blood-thinners

Refresh Me!

1 cup chilled green tea

½ peeled and pitted avocado

4 peeled and de-seeded oranges

3–4 ice cubes

Facing page: Refresh Me!
Top: Hot Saucy Mama

Infuse a teaspoon of green tea leaves in boiling water, brew, then strain, cool, and chill before adding to other ingredients.

Best anti-agers: antioxidants

Fruit Salad Ballad

½ peeled and pitted mango

¼ peeled and de-seeded papaya

½ cup strawberries

½ peeled and de-seeded cantaloupe

2 tsp chia seeds

1 tbsp yogurt

½ cup water

This delicious, nutritious smoothie will make your heart sing and your toes tap.

Best energy-boosters and anti-agers: B-group vitamins, omega-3 fats, and antioxidants

Cool Dude Dad

½ peeled and de-seeded lemon

½ peeled and de-seeded lime

2 peeled and de-seeded oranges

1 de-seeded apple

1 de-seeded pear

a small handful of baby spinach leaves

1–2 cabbage leaves

small handful of parsley

¼ cup water

3–4 ice cubes

This groovy smoothie is both refreshing and nutritious.

Best anti-agers: vitamin C and other antioxidants

Facing page: Cool Dude Dad
Top: Fruit Salad Ballad

Bright Eyes

1 peeled beet
¼ cup blueberries
1 peeled and de-seeded orange
1 small carrot
1–2 thin slices of ginger
a small handful of baby spinach leaves
stevia or other sweetener (to taste)
¼ cup water
3–4 ice cubes

Shiny, alert eyes and clear vision are signs of good health, but they can be damaged by age-related macular degeneration. Fight it with fruit and vegetables!

Best eye-boosters: antioxidants

Forever Energetic

1 peeled banana
1 peeled and pitted mango
¼ cup strawberries
1 tbsp oats
1 tbsp yogurt
½ cup almond milk
1 tbsp chia seeds

Facing page: Forever Energetic
Top: Bright Eyes

An indulgent, energy-boosting smoothie that helps ward off disease as we age. Oats are also thought to help give the skin a more youthful appearance.

Best energy-boosters: B-group vitamins, low-GI carbohydrates

Lean Green Ninja

small handful of baby spinach leaves

small handful of baby kale leaves

1 small broccoli floweret

1 de-seeded pear

1 de-seeded apple

1 peeled kiwifruit

a few leaves of mint and/or parsley

1–2 thin slices of ginger

¼ cup water

This all-green drink is a great way to get those disease-fighting, immune boosting little green warriors down in one great big delicious gulp.

Best age-beaters: antioxidants

Love Life, Drink Chocolate

2 tbsp cacao powder or nibs

1 tsp maca powder

1 peeled banana

½ cup almond milk

1 tbsp flaxseed

stevia or other sweetener to taste

The ingredients in this rich-tasting smoothie help improve brain function while also boosting energy and the immune system.

Best age-beaters: omega-3 fats, B-group vitamins, antioxidants

Facing page: Love Life, Drink Chocolate
Top: Lean Green Ninja

197

Scarborough Fair

small handful of parsley

3–4 sage leaves

1 sprig rosemary leaves

1 sprig thyme leaves

1 carrot

3 peeled and de-seeded oranges

1–2 thin slices of ginger

¼ cup water

3–4 ice cubes

orange slices to garnish

The herbs in this smoothie give an intriguing edge to the sweetness of the orange. Carrots also complement oranges very nicely, both in terms of taste and nutrition.

Best anti-agers: antioxidants

Over the Rainbow

¼ cup blueberries

¼ cup raspberries

¼ cup strawberries

1 peeled and de-seeded orange

½ peeled and pitted mango

½ peeled banana

1 de-seeded apple

1 peeled kiwifruit

½ cup water

3–4 ice cubes

Spread these fruits out on your counter before you pulverize them into oblivion. The rainbow of colors is glorious, and a marker of the age-fighting antioxidants within.

Best anti-agers: antioxidants

Facing page: Scarborough Fair
Top: Over the Rainbow

No More Pressure!

A plan to treat and reduce high blood pressure

Why all the pressure? Where does it come from? Why is it a problem? High blood pressure (hypertension) is often termed "the silent killer" because its symptoms are hardly if at all noticeable, but at the same time it predisposes us to stroke, heart attack, kidney damage, and other problems. Many of us are walking around thinking we are quite healthy, with no idea that this killer might be lurking within.

It is thought that some people are more genetically predisposed to develop hypertension than others, but for the most part it is not triggered unless aggravated by certain behaviors. Five major triggers have been identified and they each link directly to our lifestyle and eating habits. They are:

- excess weight
- alcohol
- a high-salt diet (because of its sodium content)
- stress
- sedentary lifestyle

It make sense, therefore, that adopting a lifestyle that addresses these five triggers will help prevent the onset of, and also aid the treatment of, hypertension. This means shedding excess weight, limiting or eradicating alcohol intake, avoiding foods high in salt, managing stress, and exercising. The first three triggers are directly related to nutrition and hence a healthy diet high in fruit and vegetables will help in these areas. Exercise is of huge benefit to the last two triggers, and certain foods can contribute to easing stress by helping to promote a sense of calm and well-being and also by reducing levels of the "stress hormone" cortisol in the body.

The DASH Diet

This is a catchy name for what otherwise means "Dietary Approaches to Stop Hypertension," which has been proven to effectively reduce high blood pressure. Its main principles concern:

- eating a healthy diet that is rich in vegetables, fruit, low-fat dairy foods, nuts, and whole grains.
- consuming little or no saturated fats.
- including fish for its omega-3 benefits (for vegetarians, alternatives such as flaxseed and chia seeds provide omega-3 too, but it may be worth taking fish oil supplements because of the unsurpassed omega-3 benefits fish can provide). Poultry is also recommended; chicken and turkey are both good animal sources of omega-3s.
- eliminating sugary foods, drinks, and junk food from the diet.

The diet tackles head-on the diet-related triggers listed above. It appears to work because:

- A diet high in fruit, vegetables, and fiber helps manage and reduce weight.
- A diet high in fruit, vegetables, and fiber contains lots of potassium, calcium, and magnesium, which all seem to counteract at least some of the damaging effects of salt or, more correctly, the sodium in salt. Furthermore, potassium is known for its role in normalizing blood pressure; calcium is known to help lower blood pressure; and magnesium helps regulate heartbeat and supports the cardiovascular system, which in turn helps lower blood pressure (not least because it means the heart does not need to work so

hard). Another important consideration is that magnesium helps lowers levels of the stress hormone cortisol. The body needs cortisol, and levels fluctuate over the course of the day. Aside from these normal fluctuations, levels become further elevated in stressful situations, after which they should return to normal. Unfortunately, stressful lifestyles can cause almost constantly elevated levels of cortisol in the body, which in turn elevates blood pressure, among other things.

- A diet high in omega-3 fats helps to keep the arteries flexible, free-flowing, and clear of plaque; in other words, omega-3 fats help prevent the arteries from narrowing, hardening, and causing high blood pressure.

Why Is Too Much Salt or Sodium a Problem?

Salt (sodium chloride) contains sodium, a mineral that might be expected to be healthy—and indeed a delicate balance of sodium and water in the body is essential for good health. Too much of one or the other will, however, cause problems. Too much sodium is directly linked to hypertension because it causes the body to retain water, thereby placing an extra burden on the heart and blood vessels and potentially raising blood pressure. We need only a small amount of sodium in our diets; just one teaspoon of salt contains about 2,300 mg of sodium—which, for most people, is about ten times what is needed! Most people need only about 200 mg per day. Even worse, it has been claimed that the average American eats between 3,000–3,500 mg of sodium—way, way too much. Action is needed!

And What About Nitrates?

Other widely debated compounds that appear to have a beneficial impact on high blood pressure are nitrates. Nitrates have, unfortunately, also had a long and seemingly undeserved poor reputation, due largely to their use as a preservative in some less healthy food 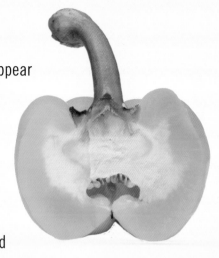 choices. But nitrates occur naturally in food and are highest of all in vegetables (nitrate is an essential nutrient for plants and is found in soil). Very importantly, the body uses nitrates to help regulate blood pressure and prevent blood clotting, among other things. Some foods high in nitrates such as beets have been shown to be particularly beneficial in this area.

In simplest terms, the body converts nitrates into either nitric oxide (healthy) or nitrosomes (unhealthy, and possibly linked to some cancers and other diseases). A diet high in fruit and vegetables will unavoidably contain nitrates, but the benefits derived from such a diet outweigh the very small risk that may be associated with nitrosomes. Vitamin C is a great helper in this area: it inhibits the production of nitrosomes. A diet rich in fruit and vegetables containing vitamin C will therefore work to counteract any potential risks posed by nitrosomes. One other important consideration when it comes to high blood pressure is that of diuretics. They are food or drinks that help rid the body of excess sodium and water, which in turn helps lower blood pressure. What makes particular fruits and vegetables more diuretic than others varies, but green watery vegetables such as celery, cucumber, and

Tip: Vitamin C inhibits the body's production of unhealthy nitrosomes.

cabbage are among the best. This is because of their high water, fiber, and mineral content. In some fruits and vegetables, this combination works in tandem with potassium and magnesium (which, as mentioned, help counteract the adverse effects of sodium) to make them especially powerful in fighting high blood pressure. Some, such as cucumbers, are also rich in sulfur, which assists the kidneys to function.

All the smoothies in this section will make a positive contribution to the dietary management of high blood pressure. To improve the benefits further, try getting up and taking a walk while sipping them, to keep the body gently active!

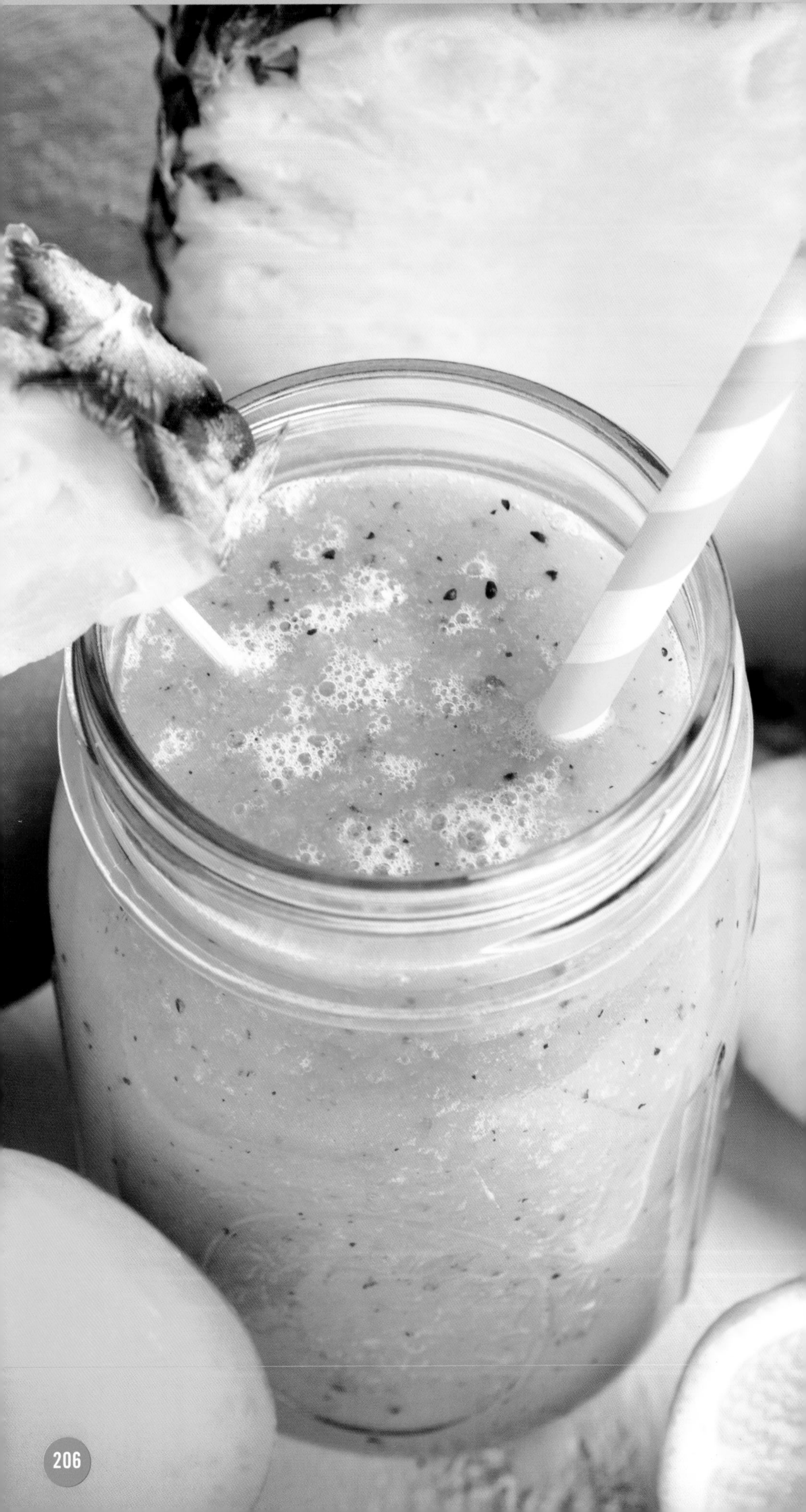

Banana Cream Dream

2 peeled bananas
¼ parsnip (root only, no leaves, ever!)
2 pitted dates
2 tbsp yogurt
stevia or other sweetener (to taste)
½ cup almond milk
3–4 ice cubes

A dreamy, delicious way to help lower blood pressure.

Best pressure-busters: potassium, magnesium, calcium

Afternoon Delight

¼ cup peeled and pitted mango
¼ cup peeled and cored pineapple
½ peeled and de-seeded lemon
1 peeled and de-seeded orange
a small handful of fresh spinach leaves
1 tablespoon flaxseed
½ cup water
3–4 ice cubes
nutmeg to garnish (optional)

What better way to relax and de-stress than sipping on this smoothie while dreaming of the Caribbean?

Best pressure-busters: potassium, magnesium, calcium, omega-3 fats

Facing page: Afternoon Delight
Top: Banana Cream Dream

Presha Busta

1 peeled beet
¼ bell pepper
1 kiwifruit
2 peeled and de-seeded oranges
½ carrot
1 tbsp chia seeds
1–2 thin slices ginger
¼ cup water
mint to garnish (optional)

This sweet-and-sour smoothie is quite thick, so if preferred replace one orange with half a cup of orange juice.

Best pressure-busters: potassium, calcium, omega-3 fats, nitrates together with vitamin C

Cool Breeze

1 peeled and de-seeded lime
½ peeled and de-seeded grapefruit
½ peeled cucumber
2 de-seeded apples
3 fresh mint leaves
1 cup water
½ cup ice cubes

This smoothie is best if kept quite watery, but use less water if a thicker smoothie is preferred.

Best pressure-busters: potassium, magnesium, calcium, diuretic properties

Facing page: Cool Breeze
Top: Presha Busta

Virgin Mary

4 tomatoes

1 stalk celery

½ peeled cucumber

½ peeled and de-seeded lemon

½ peeled and de-seeded lime

a dash low-sodium tabasco sauce

a dash low-sodium worcestershire sauce

a sprinkle of turmeric

a sprinkle of cayenne pepper

stevia or other sweetener (to taste)

leafy celery stalks for garnish

This ever-popular cocktail is of course the no-alcohol version of its even more popular cousin. Keep the amounts of tabasco and worcestershire sauce very low, and instead get your heat from the turmeric and cayenne pepper.

Best pressure-busters: potassium, magnesium, diuretic properties

Fantastic Elastic

1 tbsp flaxseed

1 tsp chia seeds

1 peeled banana

½ peeled and pitted avocado

a few small spinach leaves

1 Brazil nut

½ green apple

½ cup almond milk

stevia or other sweetener (to taste)

3–4 ice cubes

celery and lime to garnish (optional)

Rich in omega-3 fats, this smoothie helps keeps arteries clear, free-flowing, and more elastic—all very helpful for preventing or treating hypertension.

Best pressure-busters: potassium, magnesium, calcium, omega-3 fats

Facing page: Virgin Mary
Top: Fantastic Elastic

The Oasis

a small handful of parsley

2 pitted dates

½ cup peeled and cored pineapple

1 peeled and de-seeded orange

a small handful of fresh spinach leaves

1 tsp sunflower seeds

¼ cup water

½ cup ice cubes

mint for garnish (optional)

For calm among the palms.

Best pressure-busters: potassium, magnesium, calcium

Sweet Ecstasy

½ peeled and de-seeded papaya

1 peeled and pitted mango

¼ cup peeled and cored pineapple

½ cup peeled and de-seeded cantaloupe

1 tbsp flaxseed

¼ cup water

3–4 ice cubes

An exotic blend of potassium-rich tropical fruits together with a few other goodies.

Best pressure-busters: potassium, magnesium, calcium, omega-3 fats

Facing page: Sweet Ecstasy

Top: The Oasis

Royal Flush

1 peeled beet

½ peeled cucumber

1 stalk celery

2 peeled and de-seeded oranges

½ grated carrot

1–2 thin slices of ginger

a small handful parsley

stevia or other sweetener (to taste)

½ cup water

The perfect smoothie for those who like a more savory flavor.

Best pressure-busters: potassium, nitrates combined with vitamin C, diuretic properties

Kiwi Calm and Orange

1 pitted date

2 peeled kiwifruits

2 peeled and de-seeded oranges

a small handful of baby spinach leaves

1 de-seeded apple

¼ cup water

3–4 ice cubes

A particularly potassium-rich fix.

Best pressure-busters: potassium, magnesium, calcium

Facing page: Kiwi Calm and Orange
Top: Royal Flush

Captain Avocado

½ peeled avocado

1 stalk celery

½ peeled cucumber

½ cup lime juice

2 tsp olive oil (optional)

3 fresh basil leaves

2 tbsp yogurt

stevia or other sweetener (to taste)

paprika for garnish (optional)

The avocado and lime are a delicious combination that give this creamy smoothie its unique flavor. It works best if the limes are juiced beforehand—a little extra effort for a lot of extra gain.

Best pressure-busters: potassium, magnesium, calcium, diuretic properties

The Works

1 pomegranate, seeds and juice only

1 de-seeded apple

2 peeled and de-seeded oranges

½ peeled and de-seeded grapefruit

1 tbsp flaxseed

stevia or other sweetener (to taste)

¼ cup water

3–4 ice cubes

lemon for garnish (optional)

Facing page: Captain Avocado
Top: The Works

The nitrate-rich pomegranate pairs well with the grapefruit, while the orange takes the edge off the slightly tart flavors. To collect the seeds and juice from the pomegranate, cut it in half, then bash the backs sharply with the side of a wooden spoon.

Best pressure-busters: potassium, magnesium, calcium, omega-3 fats

Beauty Box

A plan to promote clear skin and healthy hair

Not only do diets high in fresh fruit and vegetables provide numerous benefits to our overall health—they also help us look good, too. Looking good might not be as important as warding off cancer and keeping the heart healthy, but it is nonetheless important for our confidence and emotional well-being—for most of us, anyway. This is especially true for adolescents as they pass through a period in their lives when feelings of self-doubt, anxiety, and insecurity may collide, wretchedly, with skin problems, and wreak further havoc upon their self esteem.

"Looking good" does not, however, need to be defined in terms of conventional notions of classic beauty, body shape, and so on. It is more about looking ourselves at our healthiest, happiest, fittest best, thereby projecting a positive energy and a sense of being happy in our own skin. This kind of vitality is enormously attractive, no matter our particular physical attributes or age. We can look good anywhere, at any age—and in a way that is determined by our individuality, not by externally prescribed standards that are both contrived and impossible to sustain over time.

Recent research has shown that some of the old beliefs regarding skin that have been variously dismissed as myths or reinstated as truth only to be dismissed again are . . . true. Junk food, greasy food, over-processed food, soda, and high-GI carbohydrates such as cake, chips, and even white bread and rice can aggravate skin conditions such as acne. On the other hand, fruit and vegetables are indeed good for the skin and promote healthy hair and nails in numerous ways.

Nature offers a boundless array of nutrients to help us to look and feel our best. There are too many to list here, but some of the big ones to consider are detailed below.

- **Water:** Present in every part of the body and essential for life itself, water helps us look healthy too. Well-hydrated skin looks plumper and fresher than less hydrated skin. Dark circles under the eyes can be a sign of dehydration, too.

- **Vitamins:** In the beauty department, vitamin C has a critical role, as it is needed for the body's production of the proteins collagen and elastin that, among other things, support and tighten our skin. Vitamins A and E are also important for supple skin and healthy hair. Vitamin B2 (riboflavin) supports healthy skin and eyes.

- **Antioxidants:** The antioxidant vitamins A, E, and C, beta-carotene, and anthocyanins all help to revitalize skin. Furthermore, anthocyanins working in conjunction with vitamin C help strengthen the collagen in skin, and this in turn may help keep wrinkles at bay as we age.

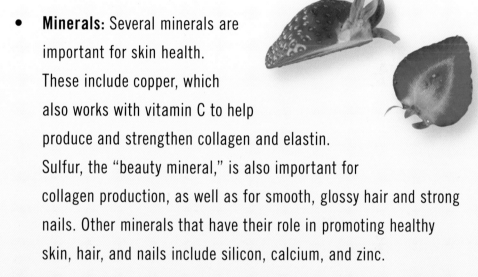

- **Minerals:** Several minerals are important for skin health. These include copper, which also works with vitamin C to help produce and strengthen collagen and elastin. Sulfur, the "beauty mineral," is also important for collagen production, as well as for smooth, glossy hair and strong nails. Other minerals that have their role in promoting healthy skin, hair, and nails include silicon, calcium, and zinc.

- **Fats:** Omega-3 fats such as those found in flaxseed and walnuts help produce the skin's natural oil barrier, which keeps skin hydrated and may even give it a healthy glow. Monounsaturated fats such as those found in avocados are also beneficial.

- **Clean, fresh air:** Over-heated or air-conditioned environments are damaging to the skin, as is smoky and otherwise stale air. Our bodies take in oxygen from fresh air, which is of course essential for our survival, but on a less critical note does mean that without enough oxygen our skin will quickly appear dull and aged. Fresh air contributes to a blooming complexion.

Peaches 'n' Cream

3 peeled and pitted peaches

2 tbsp yogurt

½ cup almond milk

stevia or other sweetener (to taste)

3–4 ice cubes

This smoothie is so delicious and nutritious that the skin tingles in anticipation.

Best skin-boosters: vitamins A, C, E, beta-carotene, calcium, copper, zinc

Cherry Baby

½ cup pitted cherries

½ cup strawberries

2 peeled and de-seeded oranges

a small handful of alfalfa sprouts

½ cup water

3–4 ice cubes

A powerful combination that helps boost collagen production. There is quite a lot of water in this recipe, for hydration purposes, but use less if you prefer a stronger flavor and thicker texture.

Best skin-boosters: antioxidants, vitamin C

Facing page: Cherry Baby
Top: Peaches 'n' Cream

Forever Young

1 pomegranate, seeds and juice only

1 tsp sesame seeds

1 peeled and de-seeded lemon

½ peeled and de-seeded apple

a small handful cabbage

½ cup water

3–4 ice cubes

A life-affirming mixture that helps support collagen and elastin production.

Best skin-boosters: copper, antioxidants, sulfur

Skin Smoother

2 tbsp yogurt

¼ cup raspberries

1 peeled banana

½ peeled and pitted mango

a small handful alfalfa sprouts

1 tsp sesame seeds

2 tbsp oats

½ cup water

3–4 ice cubes

This all-rounder has lots of the "good stuff" to help promote healthy skin, hair, and nails.

Best for healthy skin, hair, and nails: calcium, silicon, antioxidants, vitamin C, copper

Facing page: Skin Smoother
Top: Forever Young

Skin Zinger

½ cup peeled and cored pineapple

½ peeled and pitted avocado

a small handful of alfalfa sprouts

½ cup coconut water

1–2 thin slices ginger

3–4 ice cubes

parsley for garnish (optional)

An exotic smoothie with the skin-smoothing benefits of avocado combined with hydrating coconut water. Ideally, the water should be sourced directly from a fresh coconut. If using packaged coconut water, go for the highest quality and least processed.

Best skin-boosters: antioxidants, healthy fats, sulfur

Rejuvenator

2 peeled kiwifruits

¼ cup strawberries

1 peeled and de-seeded orange

½ small carrot

½ small peeled banana

a small handful of watercress

¼ cup water

3–4 ice cubes

The vitamin C and other nutrients in the fruit combine with powerful antioxidants in both the fruit and the vegetables to help rejuvenate the skin and keep the eyes healthy.

Best for healthy skin, eyes, hair, and nails: calcium, antioxidants (including lutein), sulfur, vitamin C

Facing page: Skin Zinger
Top: Rejuvenator

Cacao Butter Bliss

½ peeled and pitted avocado

2 tbsp cacao powder or nibs

1 tbsp oats

1 peeled banana

2 tbsp yogurt

stevia or other sweetener (to taste)

¼ cup water

3–4 ice cubes

This is a dreamy way to enjoy a chocolate flavor without worrying about adverse effects on the complexion. Antioxidant-rich cacao is beneficial to skin.

Best skin-boosters: antioxidants, healthy fats, sulfur

Hydrator

1 cup water

1 peeled and de-seeded apple

½ cup ice cubes

mint to garnish

This light smoothie helps hydrate the body and skin.

Best skin-boosters: water

Facing page: Hydrator
Top: Cacao Butter Bliss

Wicked Queen

1 pomegranate, seeds and juice only
½ cup pitted cherries
1 peeled and de-seeded orange
a small handful of watercress
¼ cup water
3–4 ice cubes

Just what the Wicked Queen ordered. (Snow White, eat your heart out!)

Best skin-boosters: antioxidants, vitamin C, sulfur

Wake-Up Call

2 peeled and de-seeded lemons
½ peeled cucumber
a small handful baby spinach leaves
a small handful of alfalfa
¼ cup peeled and cored pineapple
1 de-seeded apple
1–2 small slices of ginger
1 cup water
3–4 ice cubes

This sharp little number hydrates and helps cleanse the skin from the inside. It is best enjoyed, unsweetened, first thing in the morning.

Best skin-boosters: vitamin C, antioxidants, sulfur, water

Facing page: Wake-Up Call
Top: Wicked Queen

Rest and Replenish

1 cup cooled chamomile tea

1 tsp honey

1 tbsp oats

1 peeled banana

3–4 ice cubes

All skin benefits from restorative sleep. Bananas and oats contain tryptophan, an amino acid that enables the body to produce melatonin, the hormone that helps regulate the sleep cycle. Make the tea by infusing a teaspoon (or a tea bag) in boiling water. Brew for 2–3 minutes, then strain and cool.

Best skin-boosters: antioxidants

See Saw Ah-Sigh-Ee

3 oz package of frozen acai

2 peeled kiwifruits

1 peeled banana

a small handful of collard greens

1 tsp sesame seeds

¼ cup water

3–4 ice cubes

stevia or other sweetener (to taste)

mint to garnish (optional)

One of the original so-called super foods, acai (ah-sigh-ee) is packed with skin-boosting nutrients and has a slightly tart, unusual flavor that works well in smoothies.

Best skin-boosters: antioxidants, vitamin C, beta-carotene, copper

Facing page: Rest and Replenish
Top: See Saw Ah-Sigh-Ee

Red Hot Burners

A plan to boost energy and promote weight loss

Almost everyone wants a diet that not only gives them loads of energy, but also helps prevent weight gain and even encourages weight loss when needed. Maintaining a healthy weight is very important in so many ways, but in particular helps guard against, cardiovascular disease, inflammatory diseases, diabetes, and certain cancers. It also means our joints and muscles are not subjected to the burden of moving and lifting additional weight, and that our bodies are able to move around more easily and stay more flexible. And, by and large, we look and feel better about ourselves when we are a healthy weight.

Effective Weight Management

The world is awash with diets, and a great deal of confusion about them. For most people, however, a diet that follows some basic tenets, and is combined with moderate, regular exercise, will manage weight effectively. These include eating a diet that:

- is high in fresh, non-starchy vegetables and fruit.
- is moderate in low-GI carbohydrates such as whole grain cereals and starchy vegetables such as sweet potato.
- has a moderate amount of protein like legumes (these are a source of low-GI carbohydrates as well).
- is moderate in low-fat dairy and dairy alternatives.
- is low in healthy fats such as omega-3 fats.
- includes lots of fiber and water.
- restricts portion sizes.
- eliminates unhealthy fats, high-GI carbohydrates, processed foods, and alcohol, except on special occasions.
- is fundamentally balanced and nutritious, thereby providing all the nutrients our bodies need to metabolize energy.

The Importance of Nutrients

Including a moderate amount of protein in every meal is very important for at least two reasons: it keeps us feeling full for longer, and it helps to preserve muscle mass. Low-GI carbohydrates are important for sustained energy throughout the day. Legumes provide considerable protein and carbohydrates entirely on their own, but additional high-quality carbohydrates, protein, and fats can be sourced from low-GI starchy vegetables and fruits (such as sweet potato and orchard fruit), some whole grain cereals (such as oats), and high-quality fats (such as those found in avocados, nuts, and seeds). Non-starchy vegetables are low in calories and are packed with dietary fiber and an array of vitamins and minerals as well as other phytonutrients.

Do Spicy Foods Speed Up Metabolism?

People claim that some foods, especially hot foods such as chili peppers, boost metabolism and therefore also assist in weight management. It may be that certain foods do temporarily boost metabolism in this way, but not significantly, and at best only as a complement to a more comprehensive weight management program.

Do B-Group Vitamins Help?

Another caution regards the B-group vitamins; these are needed to metabolize stored energy in the body, but will not on their own bring about weight loss. Perhaps their most important role in a weight-reduction diet is that by enabling the release of energy the body feels more energetic and does more for longer. . . and thereby burns up more calories.

Put simply, vitamin B is not a significant contributor to weight loss unless it is paired with the other half of the equation, energy-needing and energy-burning activity. Exercising with weights, which helps build muscle mass, is thought to be particularly beneficial for weight loss.

The DASH Diet and the 5:2 Diet

Two diets are currently very popular and appear to be effective. The DASH diet focuses on the treatment of hypertension (see page 202) but is also effective for weight management. The 5:2 diet entails restricting calorie intake to 500 per day for women and 600 per day for men on two non-consecutive days out of seven in the week, and then eating as one pleases on the remaining five days. Smoothies fit perfectly into a 5:2 diet plan, providing a quick, satisfying, and nutritious way to sustain the body on the two low-calorie days. The plan on page 300 provides more details on this diet and is a great starting point for anyone planning to undertake a 5:2 diet for effective weight loss.

The following smoothies are designed to complement a healthy weight-reduction diet and exercise plan. They are typically high in fiber, water, and nutrients, with a particular focus on nutrients the body needs for energy and satiety, such as low-GI carbohydrates, protein, and fiber. Most of them are a meal unto themselves. And, of course, all are quick, delicious, and fun.

Please Peas Me

¼ cup fresh or frozen peas

2 peeled kiwifruits

1 de-seeded apple

1 de-seeded pear

1 tbsp flaxseed

¼ cup water

3–4 ice cubes, less if using frozen peas

mint for garnish (optional)

Peas might seem like an odd ingredient to include in a smoothie, but they have a light slightly nutty flavor that complements sweeter-flavored fruits, and they are surprisingly high in protein.

Best weight-loss helpers: protein, low-GI carbohydrates, fiber, water

Kick-Starter

1 peeled and de-seeded lemon

1 peeled and de-seeded lime

1 peeled and de-seeded orange

1 tbsp chia seeds

1–2 thin slices ginger

1 cup water

3–4 ice cubes

Try this one first thing in the morning, before breakfast, to help get things underway.

Best weight-loss helpers: vitamin C, fructose, fiber, water

Facing page: Kick-Starter
Top: Please Peas Me

Fiber Fantastic

1 tbsp flaxseed

1 tbsp sunflower seeds

1 tbsp chia seeds

1 peeled and pitted mango

2 peeled and de-seeded oranges

½ small carrot

1 cup water

3–4 ice cubes

There is no doubt that fiber helps make us feel full for longer. It also keeps the digestive system in good working order and helps prevent and cure constipation.

Best weight-loss helpers: fiber, water

Slim Jim

4 tomatoes

1 stalk celery

½ cup French beans

½ de-seeded chili pepper

1 tbsp sesame seeds

½ clove garlic

6 leaves basil

¼ cup water

A savory smoothie that works well later in the day. French beans are high in protein. The celery might also help ease bloating and fluid retention.

Best weight-loss helpers: fiber, water, capsaicin

Facing page: Slim Jim
Top: Fiber Fantastic

Morning Muesli

2 tbsp oats

2 de-seeded apples

1 de-seeded pear

1 pitted date

½ tsp cinnamon

1 tbsp flaxseed

1 tbsp yogurt

½ cup water

3–4 ice cubes

This makes for a delicious liquid breakfast, high in protein and low-GI carbs to sustain you throughout the day, together with all-important fiber.

Best weight-loss helpers: protein, low-GI carbohydrates, fiber, water

La Dolce Vita

¼ cup cannellini beans

3 tbsp cacao

1 peeled banana

½ cup almond milk

1 tbsp flaxseed

stevia or other sweetener (to taste)

3–4 ice cubes

Cannellini beans are Italian white kidney beans. They are very high in protein and fiber, and have a light subtle flavor that slips unnoticed into a smoothie but adds a lovely creamy texture. Sit back and enjoy the good life!

Best weight-loss helpers: protein, low-GI carbohydrates, fiber, vitamin C, copper

Facing page: Morning Muesli
Top: La Dolce Vita

Chocolate Rocket

1 tbsp cacao

2 tbsp yogurt

½ cup raspberries

½ cup strawberries

½ peeled banana

2 tbsp cannellini beans

½ cup almond milk

3–4 ice cubes

A delicious, high-energy, high-protein, high-fiber smoothie. To make an indulgent yet healthy mousse-like dessert, increase the yogurt to 3 tablespoons and leave out almond milk and ice cubes. Add a little sweetener if desired.

Best weight-loss helpers: protein, soluble fiber, low-GI carbohydrates

Lean and Peachy Keen

1 tbsp oats

3 peeled and pitted peaches

1 tbsp flaxseed

2 tbsp yogurt

¼ cup almond milk

stevia or other sweetener (to taste)

3–4 ice cubes

A sweet treat, perfect for earlier in the day.

Best weight-loss helpers: protein, low-GI carbohydrates, fiber

Facing page: Lean and Peachy Keen
Top: Chocolate Rocket

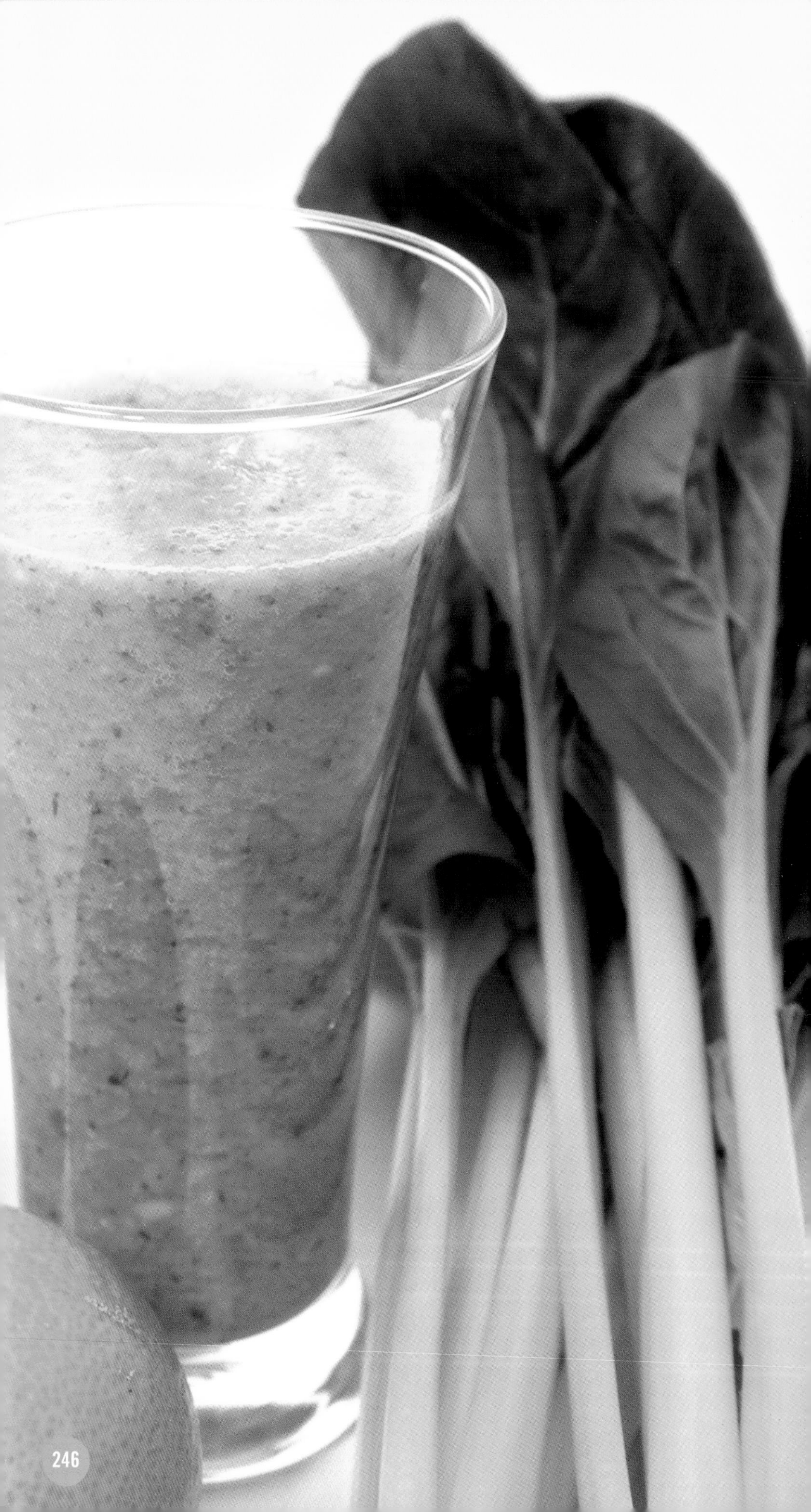

Call of the Wild

1 small handful of baby kale leaves

1 small handful of baby spinach leaves

¼ cup fresh or frozen peas

2 peeled kiwifruits

2 peeled and de-seeded oranges

¼ cup fennel

1 tbsp chia seeds

¼ cup water

3–4 ice cubes, less if using frozen peas

A good all-rounder that's full of nutrients but low in calories. It is quite thick, so replace one orange with half a cup of orange juice if desired.

Best weight-loss helpers:
low-GI carbohydrates, fiber

Bunny Hop

1 small carrot

2 peeled and de-seeded oranges

½ cup French beans

1–2 thin slices ginger

1 tbsp flaxseed

½ cup almond milk or water

3–4 ice cubes

It helps to keep the spring in your step—all day long.

Best weight-loss helpers:
low-GI carbohydrates, fiber

Facing page: Call of the Wild
Top: Bunny Hop

Smooth Moves

¼ cup cannellini beans

1 peeled banana

2 peeled kiwifruits

1 tbsp flaxseed

2 drops vanilla extract

½ cup almond milk

3–4 ice cubes

mint for garnish (optional)

A luscious smoothie that contains protein, low-GI carbohydrates, and fiber. The vanilla cuts through the creaminess of the banana and cannellini beans, and lifts the flavor. There are some claims that vanilla offers weight loss benefits of its own, but as yet they are unsubstantiated.

Best weight-loss helpers: protein, low-GI carbohydrates, fiber

Light and Breezy

1 de-seeded apple

1 peeled cucumber

3-4 leaves mint

1 tbsp flaxseed

stevia or other sweetener (to taste)

1 cup water

3–4 ice cubes

As the name suggests, a light and breezy smoothie that quenches thirst, helps keep hunger at bay between meals, and packs in loads of nutrients.

Best weight-loss helpers:
low-GI carbohydrates, fiber

Facing page: Smooth Moves
Top: Light and Breezy

Cool Moves

A plan to refresh, cool, and cleanse

The smoothies in this section are both refreshing and cooling. They might also feel in some way "cleansing," especially if integrated into a so-called "detox" diet or liquid fast. The cleansing feeling itself is a powerful motivator that encourages healthy eating and positive feelings.

The Detox Debate

Debate rages over whether detox fasts or diets provide any genuine health benefits. On one hand, healthy bodies should be capable of flushing toxins from the system very efficiently, without fasting, which itself can result in malnourishment and potentially dangerous health risks; further, fasting may lead to increased weight over time as the body switches into famine mode and slows the metabolic rate accordingly.

On the other hand, hard fasting has long been practiced in certain cultures for a variety of reasons, including medical and religious, and it seems many people do actually feel better and less sluggish after a short fast. Whether that is the power of suggestion at work, or whether they have indeed successfully detoxed, or whether they are simply carrying less semi-digested food around and hence feel lighter—or maybe a combination of all three—remains unknown.

Fasting for weight-loss or detoxification purposes is not suitable for children, adolescents, pregnant or breastfeeding women, or the elderly, and should not be undertaken by anyone—especially those with pre-existing medical conditions—without first consulting with their doctor or nutritional adviser.

Even if there is uncertainty about the long-term benefits associated with intermittent fasting or very low-calorie diets, from time to time they may have a place. If undertaken for only a short period and not too frequently, they can help give both the mind and body a rest from over-nourishment, too often a problem in our society. In reality, although there may be some weight loss (much of it water), there may be no genuine lasting benefit to the body at all. Detox diets can, however, help people shift between over-indulgence and "cleaner" eating, meaning a diet of fresh, unprocessed foods. Many people have complained of feeling sluggish and bloated after holidays and festive periods, during which they have likely fallen into a pattern of eating too much rich and over-processed food—and probably alcohol, as well. The decision to undertake a detox diet or plan for one to three days marks the stopping point for the poor diet, and heralds the healthier eating to come, and will give the liver a chance to recover from too much alcohol consumption. A little shrinking of the stomach that occurs as a result of fasting will also help curb appetite when normal eating is resumed. And, finally, some people find it difficult psychologically to make the transition from a poor diet to a nutritious one without a clean divide.

The following smoothies are intended less for fasting purposes than as refreshers and coolers. They can also be consumed on the two low-calorie days of a 5:2 diet. Page 300 provides more details on this dietary approach, together with day plans for the low-calorie days of the 5:2 diet.

Watermelon Crush

3 cups de-seeded watermelon

4 leaves mint

½ cup ice cubes

¼ cup water

This pretty pink drink is thirst-quenching and delicious.

Best cleansers: antioxidants, diuretic properties

Top: Watermelon Crush

Mint and Lime Crush

3 peeled and de-seeded limes
1 peeled and de-seeded grapefruit
a small handful of baby spinach leaves
stevia or other sweetener (to taste)
½ cup carbonated or mineral water
3–4 ice cubes

A lovely drink for a hot summer's day.

Best cleansers: antioxidants

Grapefruit and Pomegranate Zinger

3 peeled and de-seeded ruby grapefruits
1 pomegranate, seeds and juice only
¼ cup water
½ cup ice cubes

*Facing page: Grapefruit and Pomegranate Zinger
Top: Mint and Lime Crush*

The flavors of grapefruit and pomegranate complement each other beautifully in this delicious and refreshing smoothie. The more common white (or yellow) grapefruit can also be used, but gives the drink a sharper taste. If you find the taste too tart, add a little sweetener.

Best cleansers: antioxidants

Apple Teaser

3 de-seeded green apples

1 stalk celery

2 small slices ginger

¼ cup water

3–4 ice cubes

Green apples are full of nutrients and have a lovely tang that works well with the ginger and celery.

Best cleansers: antioxidants, diuretic properties

Green Tea Refresher

2 cups white grapes (frozen if possible)

1 cup strained and cooled green tea

stevia or other sweetener (to taste)

1 cup ice cubes, less if using frozen grapes

Green tea is full of antioxidants and also makes a delicious drink, hot or cold. Many claim, though it has not yet been proven, that the catechins in tea might also help boost metabolism. To make the tea, refer to page 232.

Best cleansers: antioxidants, water

Facing page: Green Tea Refresher
Top: Apple Teaser

The Rainbow

Batch 1

2 cups peeled and de-seeded honeydew

2 ice cubes and splash of water

Batch 2

2 cups peeled and de-seeded cantaloupe

2 ice cubes and splash of water

Batch 3

2 cups peeled and de-seeded watermelon

2 ice cubes and splash of water

*Facing page: Melonberry Joy (left) and
Mango Peach Sorbet
Below: The Rainbow*

This is one smoothie that takes a little more effort than usual, but is worth it for special occasions. Make each smoothie separately and place in the freezer for about 5 minutes (the smoothies need to be quite firm but not frozen). Spoon the smoothies into glasses in layers. Serve immediately.

Best cleansers: antioxidants

Mango Peach Sorbet

2 peeled and pitted mangoes

2 peeled and pitted peaches

½ cup carbonated or mineral water

1 cup ice cubes

This sweet and tangy smoothie tastes like a delicious sorbet; if you would like to serve it as a dessert, first freeze it, then allow it to soften before serving.

Best cleansers: antioxidants

Melonberry Joy

3 cups peeled and de-seeded watermelon

1 cup strawberries

¼ cup water

3–4 ice cubes

Strawberries and watermelon make a delightful combination in this refreshing drink.

Best cleansers: antioxidants, diuretic properties

Peach 'n' Pear Fizz

2 peeled and de-seeded pears

2 peeled and de-seeded peaches

1–2 small slices ginger

stevia or other sweetener (to taste)

½ cup carbonated or mineral water

3–4 ice cubes

A fizzy, fruity little number with a bit of ginger zing.

Best cleansers: antioxidants

Lemonade

5 peeled and de-seeded lemons

stevia or other sweetener (to taste)

1 cup carbonated or mineral water

1 cup ice cubes

Carbonated water or mineral water works well in blenders—just don't use too much, and open the lid carefully!

Best cleansers: antioxidants, water

Facing page: Lemonade
Top: Peach 'n' Pear Fizz

Tropical Sunset

1 peeled and de-seeded orange

1 peeled and pitted mango

½ cup peeled and cored pineapple

stevia or other sweetener (to taste)

½ cup carbonated or mineral water

3–4 ice cubes

Perfect for hot summer evenings.

Best cleansers: antioxidants

Strawberry Blush

1 cup strawberries

2 tbsp yogurt

½ cup almond milk

stevia or other sweetener (to taste)

3–4 ice cubes

Just like a strawberry milkshake!

Best cleansers: antioxidants

Facing page: Strawberry Blush
Top: Tropical Sunset

Just for Kids

A plan to meet the energy and growth needs of children

Growing kids need lots of nourishment and sustained energy through-out the day. Like adults, they need a balanced diet with plenty of fresh fruit and vegetables (2 servings of fruit and at least 5 servings of non-starchy vegetables per day); moderate amounts of protein, grains, and starchy carbohydrates; and small amounts of "good" fats, such as omega-3 fats. Depending on their age, gender, size, and level of activity, their energy needs will vary but will tend to be quite high.

Like adults, children need fiber, but not quite as much. Too much can result in filling his or her small stomach quickly, resulting in a lack of other essential nutrients. In a balanced diet, which should also include plenty of water, most children will get sufficient fiber through fruit, vegetables, and whole grains without the need for fiber supplements.

Children need all the vitamins and minerals that adults do, but have particularly high needs for calcium (for bones and teeth), vitamin D (which works with calcium to build strong bones), B-group vitamins (for metabolism, release of energy, and a healthy heart and nervous system), vitamin E (to support the immune system and to keep blood vessels healthy), iron (to help red blood cells carry oxygen around the body), and zinc (for immunity). The tables on pages 30–35 list various sources.

Children are more likely than adults to need snacks between meals, or to require six smaller meals over the course of a day rather than three. This is partly because their small stomachs may not be able to take in sufficient nutrients to sustain them between meals, and partly because, especially in energetic and fast-growing children, they may need top-ups between meals to maintain their blood sugar levels so that a drop does not cause irritability and tiredness. And they simply may feel hungry

between meals. Snacks should be nutritious, and healthy smoothies are ideal for this purpose. Unhealthy snacks such as chips, sweets, and sugary drinks should be permitted only on special occasions. Parents are not always able to control when their children eat and how much they eat, but they can assert control over what they eat while at home. This means stocking the fridge, pantry, and fruit bowl with only healthy foods, and setting a good example.

Many children don't like the taste of vegetables. Blending a few into a fruit-based smoothie is one way to introduce more of them into a child's diet, and if careful choices are made, the change in taste will be imperceptible. Spinach, for example, is wonderfully nutritious but seems to be one of the most hated vegetables among children, second only to Brussels sprouts. A few baby leaves of spinach will slip into a child's smoothie unnoticed, immediately upping its nutritional value.

Many of the recipes call for milk, and in each case either almond milk or low-fat dairy can be used. Low-fat dairy milk is an excellent choice because it is much higher in calcium than almond milk and also a good source of vitamin B12, which is so important for children. On the other hand, almond milk is generally lower in calories and is a good substitute for children who may not be able to tolerate milk. Most commercial brands of almond milk are fortified with nutrients; look for ones that contain vitamins B12, A, and E, as well as calcium and other nutrients. Other dairy milk alternatives are discussed on pages 152–53.

Smoothies are a fun way to help keep a child's diet nutritious—and they should look fun, too. Few children are likely to be willing to consume a dark green concoction that looks suspiciously like . . . liquefied spinach. A little bit of sweetener goes a long way, but only use it if necessary to introduce new flavors, and try to wean children off it as they become more accustomed to natural flavors over time. Give the drinks silly names if that helps. Here are a few to get you started.

Monkey Business

2 small bananas

2 pitted dates

1 tbsp yogurt

stevia or other sweetener (to taste)

½ cup almond or low-fat dairy milk

3–4 ice cubes

¼ teaspoon nutmeg for garnish

Most children like banana drinks—here's a yummy nutritious one that will give them an energy boost.

Best for energy and growth: carbohydrates, protein, calcium, B-group vitamins

Top: Monkey Business

Slimy Green Monster

4 peeled kiwifruits

1 de-seeded apple

handful of small spinach leaves

stevia or other sweetener, to taste

½ cup water

½ cup ice cubes

mint for garnish

So icky it must be delicious!

Best for energy: carbohydrates

Appattack

3 de-seeded apples

½ stalk celery

stevia or other sweetener, to taste

¼ cup carbonated or mineral water

½ cup ice cubes

An apple (or three) a day keeps the doctor away.

Best for energy: carbohydrates

Facing page: Slimy Green Monster
Top: Appattack

Chocolate Milkshake

2 tbsp cacao

a small handful of baby spinach leaves

2 tbsp yogurt

stevia or other sweetener, to taste

½ cup almond or low-fat dairy milk

3–4 ice cubes

berries for garnish

This delicious smoothie tastes just like a chocolate milkshake but has lots of extra nutrients, including some fiber in the spinach.

Best for energy and growth: calcium, B-group vitamins

Pretty in Pink

1 cup strawberries

2 tbsp yogurt

½ cup almond or low-fat dairy milk

stevia or other sweetener, to taste

3–4 ice cubes

Facing page: Chocolate Milkshake
Top: Pretty in Pink

This dreamy strawberry smoothie is a delight to behold as well as to drink.

Best for energy and growth: calcium, B-group vitamins

Orange and Mango Spider

Ingredients for the syrup

1 tbsp honey

1 orange, juice only

¼ cup water

Ingredients for the smoothie

1 peeled and pitted mango

1 peeled and de-seeded orange

½ small carrot

2 tbsp plain frozen yogurt

1 cup carbonated or mineral water

You'll need to make the syrup first, but it's easy, and any left over will keep in the fridge for a day or two.

Bring syrup ingredients to a boil in a saucepan. Boil for ten minutes, stirring occasionally, or until the mixture has a light syrupy texture. Cool. Blend mango, orange, carrot, water, and a tablespoon of syrup in the blender. Pour into a tall glass. Top with the frozen yogurt, followed by a splash of carbonated (or mineral) water and a few drops of extra syrup to finish.

Best for energy and growth:

carbohydrates, calcium, B-vitamins

Facing page: Oranges and Lemons
Below: Orange and Mango Spider

Oranges and Lemons

2 peeled and de-seeded lemons

2 peeled and de-seeded oranges

½ carrot

a small handful of cabbage leaves

½ cup carbonated or mineral water

3–4 ice cubes

A popular blend of flavors as enduring as the nursery rhyme of old ("Oranges and lemons, say the bells of St. Clement's. . .")

Best for growth:

B-group vitamins, vitamin K

273

Orange Fizz

4 peeled and de-seeded oranges

½ small carrot

¼ cup carbonated or mineral water

3–4 ice cubes

A refreshing and energizing variation of a favorite fruit-and-vegetable blend.

Best for energy and growth: vitamin C, B-group vitamins, natural sugars

Raspberry Ripper

2 cups raspberries

1 small peeled beet

stevia or other sweetener, to taste

½ cup coconut water or water

3–4 ice cubes

It is very easy to sneak in a beet—or two—into this lovely raspberry smoothie.

Best for energy and growth: B-group vitamins, vitamin A

Facing page: Manana Bango
Top: Raspberry Ripper (left) and Orange Fizz

Manana Bango

1 peeled and pitted mango
1 peeled banana
1 tbsp oats
 1 tbsp yogurt
½ cup almond milk
nutmeg and lemon slice for garnish

This high-energy smoothie makes for a great start to the day.

Best for energy and growth: carbohydrates, calcium, B-group vitamins

Chocaberry Blitz

2 tbsp cacao

1 tbsp cannellini beans

½ cup strawberries

½ cup raspberries

stevia or other sweetener, to taste

½ cup almond or low-fat dairy milk

3–4 ice cubes

The beans give this smoothie a luscious, creamy texture and a protein boost, without changing the chocolate-and-berry flavor.

Best for energy and growth:
B-group vitamins, calcium, protein

Tutti Frutti

¼ cup peeled and cored pineapple

1 peeled and de-seeded orange

1 peeled and de-seeded lemon

1 de-seeded apple

1 peeled kiwifruit

½ peeled and de-seeded ruby grapefruit

small handful of baby spinach leaves

¼ cup carbonated or mineral water

3–4 ice cubes

A fruity concoction designed to delight and energize.

Best for energy and growth:
vitamin C, natural sugars

Facing page: Tutti Frutti
Top: Chocaberry Blitz

277

Sleep Easy

A plan to encourage restful, restorative sleep

A good night's sleep is essential to health. During sleep, our bodies and our minds are rested and restored. Sleep also has a role in weight control because insufficient sleep can affect two hunger hormones, ghrelin and leptin, which in turn can lead to overeating. Ghrelin tells our brains when it is time to eat; when we are sleep-deprived, our bodies produce more of it, causing us to eat more, and more often. Leptin, on the other hand, tells us when we've had enough to eat. When we are sleep-deprived, our bodies don't produce enough, so we don't know to stop eating. An additional problem arises with the stress hormone cortisol. Our bodies produce more of it when we haven't had adequate sleep, and in response our bodies begin to conserve energy, causing our metabolism to slow down and increasing the likelihood of excess nutrients being stored as fat rather than being used for energy. But for some people, sleep is elusive and they stay awake for much of the night; for others, they may fall asleep, only to awaken a little while later. And for some, their sleep is not restful, and is disturbed by twitching muscles and conditions such as restless leg syndrome. Diet does not provide the answer to all these questions, but it can help. Some common suggestions include:

- Avoid alcohol. Although some may find alcohol lulls them to sleep more easily, the quality of sleep is generally poor and, because alcohol is a diuretic, it can result in many wake-up calls of nature that will in turn disrupt the quality of sleep.
- Avoid heavy meals in the evening. Full meals should not be consumed within two hours of going to bed.
- A small, light snack or drink before bed can help bring slumber. This is especially so if the food contains tryptophan, such as milk or

bananas. The tryptophan is converted to serotonin in the body, which helps calm the mind and prepare it for sleep.

- Avoid caffeine drinks after 4pm if you are caffeine-sensitive or a slow metabolizer of caffeine.
- Enjoy some form of moderate exercise during the day.
- Try using a few drops of aromatic scents such as lavender on your pillow—many people find this helpful.

Foods that seem to help people achieve a good night's sleep include:

- Milk, bananas, spinach, oats, sunflower seeds, and sesame seeds. They contain the amino acid tryptophan, which increases the level of serotonin in the brain. Serotonin promotes calm and serenity that in turn may help induce sleep. The hormone melatonin is also produced by the body from tryptophan (serotonin is converted to melatonin). Melatonin regulates the body's internal clock, including wake and sleep cycles.
- Chamomile tea, which many claim promotes relaxation and calm, and helps induce sleep.
- Honey, which many people find has a calming effect. Some claim that if combined with chamomile tea it is particularly soporific. This has not yet been scientifically proven, but may be worth a try!
- Magnesium has been shown to be effective in the treatment of restless legs syndrome, which is very disruptive to sleep. Magnesium is also thought to help bring about sleep in various other, not yet fully understood, ways.
- Foods that contain inositol, a vitamin-like substance found in some foods such as cantaloupe, some legumes, and raisins. It is thought to help with anxiety and insomnia, among other things. Foods containing inositol—cantaloupe is a particularly rich source—may therefore assist in bringing about sleep.

Rest and Restore

1 tsp honey

1 tbsp oats

1 peeled banana

a drop or two vanilla extract

½ cup almond milk

Top: Rest and Restore

Bananas and oats are rich in tryptophan, which enables the body to produce both serotonin and melatonin and hence may help encourage a restful sleep.

Best sleep-inducers: tryptophan

Sleepy Tea

1 cup cooled and strained chamomile tea

1 tbsp sesame seeds

1 tsp honey

Chamomile tea blended with a little honey has long been used in folk medicine to help induce sleep. Some studies suggest that it may indeed help relieve anxiety, which in turn assists with sleep. It might work for you! You will need to make the tea beforehand (see page 232).

Best sleep-inducers: tryptophan

Blissful Slumber

a few baby spinach leaves

¼ peeled and de-seeded cantaloupe

1 peeled banana

1 tbsp sesame seeds

1 tbsp yogurt

½ cup almond milk

A lovely, creamy, pre-sleep smoothie.

Best sleep-inducers: tryptophan, inositol

Sweet Dreams

¼ peeled and de-seeded cantaloupe

½ peeled and pitted mango

½ cup strawberries

1 tbsp sesame seeds

½ cup almond milk

A dreamy sleep-inducer . . .

Best sleep-inducers: tryptophan, inositol

Facing page: Sleepy Tea (top) and Blissful Slumber
Top: Sweet Dreams

Sleepy Head

3 peeled kiwifruits
½ peeled and pitted avocado
1 tbsp oats
stevia or other sweetener, to taste
½ cup almond milk

Kiwifruit contains tryptophan, which is thought to help induce sleep. Preliminary research has also shown that kiwifruit appears to improve sleep onset, duration, and quality. Avocado is also high in tryptophan.

Best sleep-inducers: tryptophan, inositol

"Chocolate" Nightcap

2 tbsp raw carob powder
1 pitted date
1 peeled banana
stevia or other sweetener, to taste
½ cup almond milk

This smoothie uses carob instead of cacao to create chocolate-like flavor without the stimulants caffeine and theobromine. Almond milk can be slightly warmed beforehand, up to 110°F if preferred, without compromising the nutrients significantly.

Best sleep-inducers: tryptophan, inositol

Facing page: Sleepy Head
Top: "Chocolate" Nightcap

Wiggly Legs No More

a few baby spinach leaves

1 tbsp sesame seeds

1 tbsp cannellini beans

1 peeled banana

½ peeled and de-seeded cantaloupe

½ cup almond milk

The nutrients in this smoothie might help settle restless legs and induce calm, restful sleep.

Best sleep-inducers: tryptophan, inositol, magnesium

Moonlit Night

¼ cup dried goji berries

½ cup pitted cherries

a few baby spinach leaves

¼ cup blueberries

1 pitted date

1 tsp honey

½ cup water

This smoothie includes the nutrient-rich goji berry together with cherries, a natural source of melatonin.

Best sleep-inducers: magnesium, tryptophan

Facing page: Wiggly Legs No More
Top: Moonlit Night

All-Rounders

A few more nourishing smoothies to revive and inspire

Beet and Berry Blast

¼ cup strawberries

¼ cup raspberries

¼ cup blueberries

1 small peeled beet

1 tbsp yogurt

1 peeled and de-seeded orange

stevia or other sweetener, to taste

¼ cup water

3–4 ice cubes

Fog Buster

½ cup baby kale leaves

1 cup fresh or frozen blueberries

½ peeled banana

1 tbsp flaxseed

½ cup green tea, strained and cooled

½ cup almond milk

4 ice cubes (less if using frozen berries)

Sky's the Limit

½ cup baby spinach leaves

2 tbsp cacao

1 tbsp powdered maca

½ peeled banana

1 tbsp flaxseed

½ cup almond milk

3–4 ice cubes

Green Machine

1 cup baby spinach leaves

1 tbsp yogurt

1–2 thin slices ginger

1 peeled and pitted avocado

¼ cup water

3–4 ice cubes

Top: Beet and Berry Blast
Left: Green Machine

Good Morning, Sunshine

½ de-seeded bell pepper

2 peeled and de-seeded oranges

½ cup peeled and cored pineapple

a small handful of baby spinach leaves

1 small carrot

½ cup water

3–4 ice cubes

Beetle Juice

3 peeled beets

1 small carrot

1 celery stalk with leaves

1 peeled and de-seeded orange

1 de-seeded apple

1–2 thin slices ginger

½ cup water

3–4 ice cubes

Feeling Fantastic

½ cup pineapple

½ peeled and pitted mango

1 peeled and de-seeded orange

½ cup frozen blueberries

1 tbsp frozen acai pulp

½ cup frozen raspberries

½ cup ice

mint, for garnish

Purée the first three ingredients together with half the ice. Pour into glass. Rinse blender thoroughly then purée the remaining ingredients except the mint. Pour this second blend into the glass, on top of the first. Top with finely chopped mint and a few seeds.

Right: Feeling Fantastic

In the Limelight

4 peeled and de-seeded limes

1 peeled kiwifruit

1 peeled and de-seeded orange

a small handful of baby spinach leaves

¼ cup water

stevia or other sweetener, to taste

3–4 ice cubes

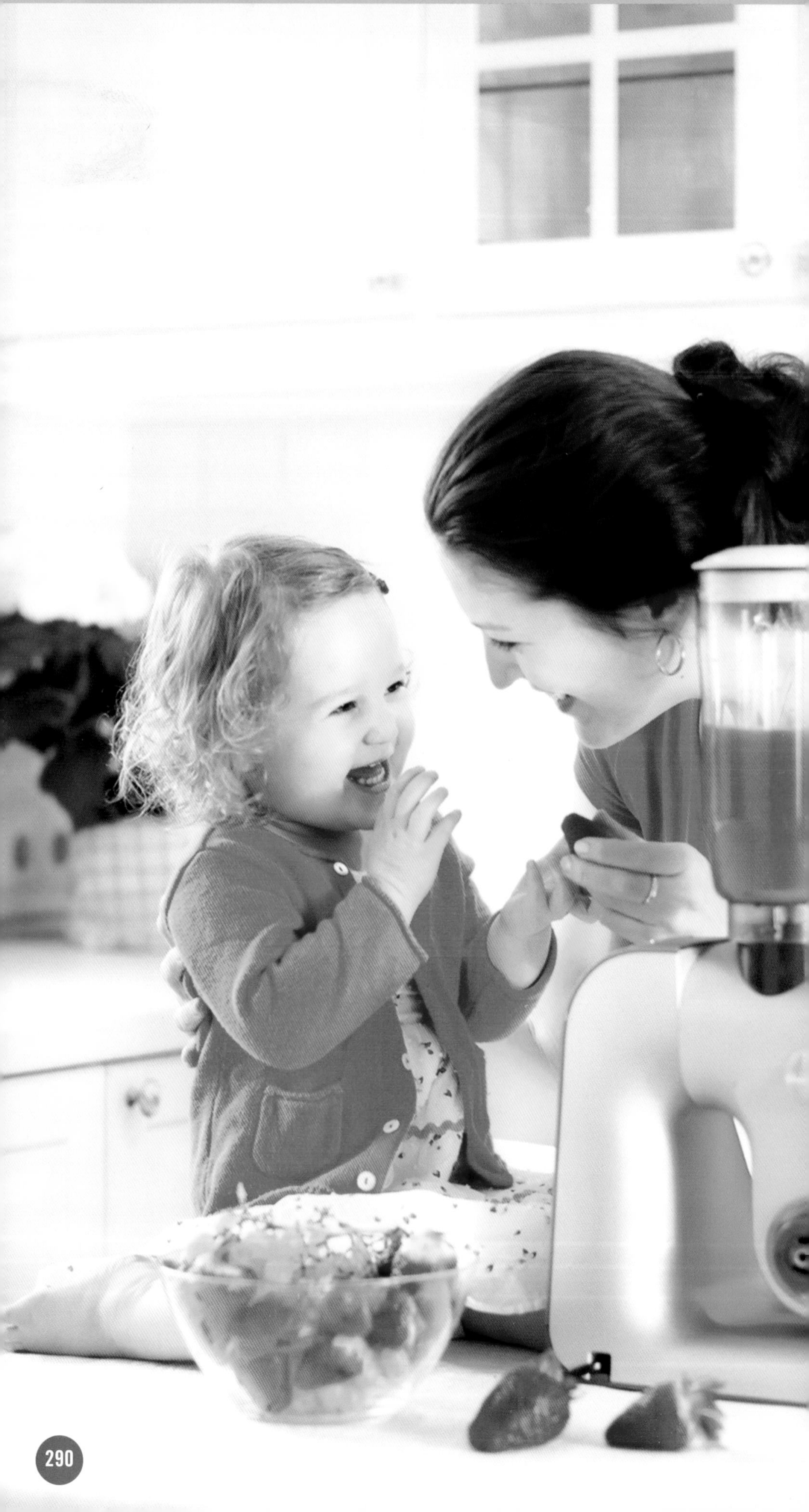

Healthy Eating
PLANS

The following healthy recipes and eating plans correspond to seven of the eight sections in this book: Happy Days, Fountain of Youth, No More Pressure!, Beauty Box, Red Hot Burners, Cool Moves, and Just for Kids. There is not a plan for the Sleep Easy section, which is more general in nature.

With the exception of Cool Moves and Red Hot Burners, each plan is in accordance with the Dietary Guidelines for Americans and provides approximately 2,000 calories per day. This will meet the needs of a moderately active adult female, but males may require an extra 200 to 400 calories. This can be achieved by increasing quantities by 10 to 20 percent, or simply by adding the following each day:

200 extra calories: 1 piece of fruit, 5 oz low-fat yogurt, and 2 tsp of nuts

400 extra calories: 2 pieces of fruit, 2 slices of grainy bread with 1½ oz (or 3 tbsp shredded) reduced-fat cheese, and 1 oz lettuce.

If weight loss is not your goal, be guided by your hunger. The Cool Moves and Red Hot Burner plans do not meet the guidelines due to their limited number of calories. As always, please consult with your medical practitioner if you have specific dietary or medical needs.

Note for Vegetarians: See page 304 for vegetarian alternatives to fish and poultry ingredients.

Happy Days

7-Day Mood-Boosting Plan

Day 1

Breakfast
- Bananaberry Bonanza (p. 174)
- 2 slices grainy toast with 2 tsp nut spread
- 3 tbsp goji berries

Lunch
- Easy As ABC (p. 173)
- 3 large multigrain crackers
- 1 tbsp reduced-fat cheese
- 1 sliced tomato
- ½ cup watercress

Dinner
- Poached Chicken with Italian Tomatoes (p. 308)
- 1 slice grainy sourdough bread
- 1 cup steamed asparagus
- 1 cup steamed green beans topped with 2 tsp toasted sesame seeds

Snacks
- 1 cup low-fat natural yogurt
- 3 cups air-popped popcorn
- 2 cups cubed melon
- 1 skim-milk caffe latte

Day 2

Breakfast
- Bircher Muesli with Berries (p. 304)

Lunch
- Beet, Beet, Beetin' the Blues (p. 177)
- 3 whole-grain wraps filled with 3 tbsp avocado, 3 oz canned tuna (in springwater, drained), 1 sliced cucumber, and a few parsley leaves

Dinner
- Spiced Chickpeas and Pumpkin (p. 312)

Snacks
- Mango Tango (p. 173)
- ⅔ cup low-fat natural yogurt
- 1 apple
- 1 kiwifruit

Day 3

Breakfast
- 3-B-Baby (p. 174)
- 2 slices grainy toast topped with 2 tbsp reduced-fat ricotta cheese
- 1 de-seeded sliced pear

Lunch
- Flax Attack (p. 181)
- Green Salad (p. 307)
- 2 cups watermelon

Dinner
- Spaghetti with Prawns and Spinach (p. 311)

Snacks
- ⅔ cup low-fat natural yogurt
- 3 cups air-popped popcorn
- 3 Brazil nuts
- 4 dates
- 1 skim-milk caffe latte

Day 4

Breakfast

- Good Morning Kale (p. 181)
- 2 slices grainy toast topped with 2 tbsp avocado and 2 tbsp reduced-fat cheese

Lunch

- Bean Thread Noodle Salad with Poached Chicken (p. 304)

Dinner

- Crisp Vegetable and Tofu Stir-Fry (p. 306)

Snacks

- Mangoberrylicious (p. 177)
- ⅔ cup low-fat natural yogurt
- 1 pear
- 2 kiwifruits

Day 5

Breakfast

- Open Sesame (p. 178)
- ½ cup natural muesli served with ½ cup skim milk
- ⅓ cup low-fat natural yogurt
- 1 cup berries

Lunch

- Kiwi-Kale-a-Cado (p. 178)
- 3 multigrain crackers topped with 1 tbsp reduced fat cheese, 1 sliced tomato, and 1 cup arugula

Dinner

- Poached Mackerel (p. 309)
- Sweet and Tasty Brown Rice Salad (p. 313)

Snacks

- ⅔ cup low-fat natural yogurt

Day 6

Breakfast

- 2 slices grainy toast topped with 2 poached eggs
- 2 cups mushrooms sautéed in 2 tsp olive oil
- 1 cup baby spinach
- 1 skim-milk caffe latte

Lunch

- Nutrition Bomb (p. 182)
- 1 cup berries
- 1 pear
- 3 Brazil nuts

Dinner

- Moroccan Chickpea and Quinoa Chicken Salad (p. 308)

Snacks

- 3-B-Baby
- 1 cup low-fat natural yogurt
- 3 cups air-popped popcorn
- 2 kiwifruits

Day 7

Breakfast

- Chocolate Wonderland (p. 182)
- 1 apple

Lunch

- Beet, Beet, Beetin' the Blues (p. 177)
- 3 large multigrain crackers topped with 3 tbsp avocado and 3 oz canned tuna (in springwater, drained)

Dinner

- Spiced Farro and Eggplant Salad (p. 312)

Snacks

- ⅔ cup low-fat natural yogurt
- 1 cup berries
- 1 skim-milk caffe latte

Fountain of Youth

7-Day Plan for Cardiovascular and Brain Health

Day 1

Breakfast
- 123–O.M.G. (p. 189)
- 1 slice grainy toast topped with
  1 tsp honey, 1 sliced banana, and
  1 tsp chia seeds

Lunch
- Bright Eyes (p. 194)
- 3 multigrain crackers with 3 tbsp
  hummus and 1 sliced cucumber
- 1 cup red grapes

Dinner
- Soba Noodles with Marinated Salmon
  and Greens (p. 311)

Snacks
- 1 cup low-fat natural yogurt
- 1 orange
- 1 skim-milk caffe latte

Day 2

Breakfast
- 2 slices grainy toast topped with 1 egg
  cooked with 1 tsp olive oil in a nonstick
  pan, and 4½ oz baked beans
- 1 cup orange juice

Lunch
- Brain Train (p. 189)
- ⅔ cup low-fat natural yogurt
- 1 apple

Dinner
- Hot Saucy Mama (p. 190)
- Watercress Salad with Chicken, Pear, and
  Walnuts (p. 315)

Snacks
- 1 cup skim milk
- 1¾ oz fruit and nut trail mix/granola bar
- 3 cups air-popped popcorn

Day 3

Breakfast
- Forever Energetic (p. 194)

Lunch
- 3 whole-grain wraps filled with 3 oz tuna
  (in springwater, drained), 2 tbsp avocado,
  and 1 cup sliced cherry tomatoes
- 1 skim-milk caffe latte
- 1 cup berries

Dinner
- Fettucini with Sweet Onion and Kale
  (p. 307)

Snacks
- Cool Dude Dad (p. 193)
- ⅔ cup low-fat natural yogurt

Day 4

Breakfast

- Over the Rainbow (p. 199)
- 1 tbsp sunflower seeds
- 1½ tbsp goji berries
- 1½ tbsp currants

Lunch

- 1 cup skim milk with 1 tbsp cacao and 1 tsp maple syrup
- 3 grainy crackers with 1 tbsp nut spread
- 1 pear

Dinner

- Lean Green Ninja (p. 197)
- Tuna Nicoise Salad (p. 314)
- 1 slice grainy bread

Snacks

- 1 cup low-fat natural yogurt

Day 5

Breakfast

- Love Life, Drink Chocolate (p. 197)

Lunch

- 3 large multigrain crackers with 2 tbsp reduced-fat cheese and 1 sliced tomato
- 1 cup mixed berries
- ½ cup orange juice

Dinner

- Chili Tomato Spaghetti (p. 305)
- 1 glass red wine

Snacks

- Fruit Salad Ballad (p. 193)
- ⅔ cup low-fat natural yogurt
- 1 English muffin with 2 tsp berry jam

Day 6

Breakfast

- 2 slices grainy toast topped with 1 egg and 1 cup mushrooms cooked in 1 tsp olive oil
- 1 skim-milk caffe latte

Lunch

- Forever Energetic (p. 194)
- Grainy-bread sandwich made with 1¾ oz shaved chicken breast, 1 tbsp avocado, 1 tbsp reduced-fat cheese
- 1 cup arugula

Dinner

- Pumpkin, Chickpea, and Beet Couscous (p. 310)

Snacks

- Scarborough Fair (p. 198)
- ⅔ cup low-fat natural yogurt

Day 7

Breakfast

- Brain Train (p. 189)
- 1 slice grainy toast with 1 tbsp reduced-fat cheese

Lunch

- 3 large multigrain crackers with 3 tbsp hummus and 3 oz canned tuna (in springwater, drained)
- 1 skim-milk caffe latte

Dinner

- Rattatouille (p. 310)

Snacks

- Refresh Me! (p. 190)
- 5 pecan halves
- 1 cup blueberries
- ⅔ cup low-fat natural yogurt

No More Pressure!

7-Day Plan for Hypertension Prevention and Treatment

Day 1

Breakfast

- Banana Cream Dream (p. 207)
- 1 slice whole grain bread with
  1 tsp 100% fruit jam

Lunch

- Raw Beet and Chickpea Salad (p. 310)
- 1 apple
- 1 skim-milk caffe latte

Dinner

- Poached Salmon and Ginger (p. 309)
- Garden Salad (p. 307)
- 5 oz steamed potatoes

Snacks

- Afternoon Delight (p. 207)
- 1 pear
- 1 tbsp goji berries
- ⅔ cup low-fat
  natural yogurt

Day 2

Breakfast

- Bircher Muesli with Apple (p. 304)
- 1 cup orange juice

Lunch

- Fantastic Elastic (p. 211)
- 1 sliced pear
- ⅔ cup low-fat natural yogurt

Dinner

- Vegetable Frittata (p. 314)
- Snow Pea Salad (p. 311)
- 1 grainy dinner roll

Snacks

- Royal Flush (p. 215)
- 3 cups air-popped popcorn
- 1 skim-milk caffe latte
- 2 kiwifruits

Day 3

Breakfast

- 1 slice grainy toast topped with 1 tbsp
  ricotta cheese and 1 fresh peach
- 2 cups strawberries
- 1½ tbsp golden raisins
- 1 skim-milk caffe latte

Lunch

- Captain Avocado (p. 216)
- 3 grainy biscuits topped with 1 tbsp
  hummus, 3 oz canned tuna (in springwater,
  drained), and 1 cup arugula
- 1 apple

Dinner

- Zucchini Basil Pasta (p. 315)
- 1 grainy dinner roll

Snacks

- Cool Breeze (p. 208)
- 1 cup diced melon
- ⅔ cup low-fat natural yogurt
- 3 tbsp dried goji berries

Day 4

Breakfast
- Kiwi Calm and Orange (p. 215)
- 1 slice grainy toast topped with 1 sliced banana, 1 tsp honey, and 1 tsp chia seeds

Lunch
- Grainy sandwich with 1 tbsp avocado, 1 tbsp reduced-fat cheese, 1 small sliced cucumber, 1 small grated beet, and 1 cup lettuce leaves
- 1 skim-milk caffe latte
- 2 kiwifruits

Dinner
- Poached Chicken with Quinoa, Almonds, and Pear (p. 309)

Snacks
- Virgin Mary (p. 210)
- 2 cups carrot and celery strips served with 2 tbsp hummus
- ⅔ cup low-fat natural yogurt
- 1 tbsp sunflower seeds
- 3 cups air-popped popcorn

Day 5

Breakfast
- Sweet Ecstasy (p. 212)
- 1 slice grainy toast with 1 tbsp avocado and 1 poached egg

Lunch
- Spiced Chickpea Couscous (p. 312)
- 1 skim-milk caffe latte
- 1 small pear

Dinner
- Prawn Stir-Fry with Wild Rice (p. 309)

Snacks
- Presha Busta (p. 208)
- 1 cup low-fat natural yogurt
- 1½ tbsp goji berries
- 2 tsp chia seeds
- 1 banana

Day 6

Breakfast
- ½ cup natural muesli with ½ cup skim milk
- ⅓ cup low-fat natural yogurt with 1 cup mixed berries
- 1 cup orange juice

Lunch
- Fantastic Elastic (p. 211)
- 1 multigrain rice cake with 1 tbsp hummus
- 2 cups carrot and celery strips

Dinner
- Farro and Lentil Salad (p. 306)

Snacks
- The Oasis (p. 212)
- 1 cup low-fat natural yogurt
- 1 cup melon cubes
- 1 apple

Day 7

Breakfast
- The Works (p. 217)
- 1 slice grainy toast with 1 cup button mushrooms cooked in 1 tsp olive oil and drizzled with balsamic vinegar

Lunch
- Banana Cream Dream (p. 207)
- 3 large grainy crackers with ¼ cup cottage cheese, 1 sliced cucumber, and 1 cup arugula

Dinner
- Poached Mackerel with Mango Salsa (p. 309)
- Vietnamese Rice Noodle Salad (p. 314)

Snacks
- 1 cup low-fat natural yogurt
- 1½ tbsp goji berries
- 2 tsp sunflower seeds
- 2 tsp pumpkin seeds
- ½ peeled and pitted mango

Beauty Box

7-Day Plan for Clear, Beautiful Skin

Day 1

Breakfast
- Peaches 'n' Cream (p. 223)
- 1 cup natural muesli with ½ cup skim milk
- ⅓ cup low-fat natural yogurt

Lunch
- Soy-and-linseed bread sandwich with 2 tbsp avocado, 3 oz canned tuna (in springwater, drained), and 1 sliced tomato
- 1 ruby grapefruit

Dinner
- 6 oysters with a squeeze of fresh lime juice
- Stir-Fried Tofu and Greens (p. 313)
- ⅓ cup brown rice cooked according to package instructions

Snacks
- Hydrator (p. 228)
- ⅔ cup low-fat natural yogurt

Day 2

Breakfast
- Cherry Baby (p. 223)
- ¾ cup whole grain cereal with ½ cup skim milk, ⅓ cup low-fat natural yogurt, and 1 cup strawberries

Lunch
- Forever Young (p. 224)
- Soy-and-linseed bread sandwich with 1 tbsp nut spread and 1 sliced banana

Dinner
- Poached Salmon (p. 309)
- Nutty Sweet Potato (p. 308)
- Balsamic Salad (p. 304)

Snacks
- ⅔ cup low-fat natural yogurt
- 1 cup blueberries
- 1 cup peeled and cored pineapple
- 5 almonds

Day 3

Breakfast
- Rejuvenator (p. 227)
- 2 slices soy-and-linseed toast with 1 sliced tomato and 2 tbsp reduced-fat cheese

Lunch
- Skin Smoother (p. 224)
- 1¾ oz fruit and nut trail mix/granola bar
- 1 cup red grapes

Dinner
- Wild Rice Salad with Chickpeas and Mango (p. 315)

Snacks
- 1 cup low-fat natural yogurt with 2 tbsp wheat germ and 10 roughly chopped almonds stirred in

Day 4

Breakfast
- Cacao Butter Bliss (p. 228)
- 1 slice grainy toast with 1 poached egg and 1 cup mushrooms cooked in 1 tsp olive oil

Lunch
- Brown Rice with Tuna and Kidney Beans (p. 305)
- 1 grapefruit

Dinner
- Zucchini Linguini (p. 315)

Snacks
- Rest and Replenish (p. 232)
- ⅔ cup low-fat natural yogurt
- 1 skim-milk caffe latte

Day 5

Breakfast

- See Saw Ah-Sigh-Ee (p. 233)
- 1 slice crusty sourdough toast topped with 2 tbsp avocado, 1 sliced tomato, 1 tbsp reduced-fat feta cheese, small handful of watercress, a few basil leaves, and drizzled with 1 tsp olive oil

Lunch

- Wicked Queen (p. 231)
- 3 large multigrain crackers topped with 3 tbsp hummus and 1 sliced cucumber
- 1 cup mixed berries

Dinner

- Poached Mackerel (p. 309)
- Potato and Parsnip Mash (p. 308)
- Chili Swiss Chard (p. 305)
- 1 cup each steamed carrot and snow peas topped with 1 tsp toasted sesame seeds

Snacks

- 1 cup low-fat natural yogurt
- 1 cup diced papaya
- 3 tbsp golden raisins
- 1 skim-milk caffe latte

Day 6

Breakfast

- Wake-Up Call (p. 231)
- Bircher Muesli with Apple, Cinnamon, and Almonds (p. 304)

Lunch

- Cacao Butter Bliss (p. 228)
- 1 grainy bread roll with 2 oz shaved chicken, small handful of baby spinach leaves, 1 sliced spring onion, and ¼ sliced, peeled, and pitted mango
- ⅔ cup low-fat natural yogurt

Dinner

- Red Bell Pepper and Spinach Omelet (p. 310)
- 1 cup lettuce mixed with 1 sliced cucumber and 1 cup yellow cherry tomatoes
- 1 slice crusty sourdough bread
- 1 cup orange juice

Snacks

- 1 cup skim milk
- 1 cup red grapes
- 1 cup berries
- 2 multigrain rice cakes

Day 7

Breakfast

- Forever Young (p. 224)
- ⅔ cup low-fat natural yogurt with 2 tbsp wheat germ topped with 1 tbsp sunflower seeds and 1 cup strawberries

Lunch

- Soy-and-linseed bread sandwich with 2 tbsp hummus, ½ grated raw beet, ½ grated carrot, and 1 cup arugula
- 1 cup peeled and diced papaya
- 1 cup apple and guava juice
- 3 Brazil nuts

Dinner

- Smoked Salmon and Dill Frittata (p. 311)
- 1 cup lettuce mixed with 1 chopped cucumber and 1 tbsp avocado

Snacks

- Skin Smoother (p. 224)
- 1 skim-milk caffe latte
- 3 rye crackers with 1 tbsp reduced-fat cheese and 1 sliced tomato

Red Hot Burners

4-Week Metabolism and Weight Management Plan

These 2-day weight loss plans have been designed to fit what's known as a 5:2 diet. They provide 500 calories per day (approximately 25 percent of the usual daily intake for a moderately active female—see page 291). Males may need to increase this to 600 calories, which can be achieved by adding any one of the following to each day:

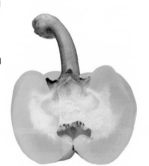

- ⅔ cup low-fat yogurt and 1 cup of vegetable sticks
- 1 piece of fruit and 2 tsp nuts
- 2 small eggs

Quantities may be further reduced or increased according to your specific needs. The 2-day plans should be followed for 2 non-consecutive days out of every 7, with normal (non-restricted) eating on the remaining 5 days.

WEEK 1	Day 1	Day 2

Breakfast
- Morning Muesli (p. 242)

Dinner
- ⅔ cup low-fat natural yogurt
- 1 cup celery strips

Breakfast
- Kick-Starter (p. 239)

Dinner
- Please Peas Me (p. 239)

WEEK 2	Day 1	Day 2

Breakfast
- Fiber Fantastic (p. 240)

Dinner
- ⅔ cup low-fat natural yogurt

Breakfast
- Call of the Wild (p. 247)

Dinner
- Light and Breezy (p. 249)
- 1 cup broccoli florets

WEEK 3	Day 1	Day 2

Breakfast
- Bunny Hop (p. 247)

Dinner
- Slim Jim (p. 240)
- 1 cup carrot strips

Breakfast
- Lean and Peachy Keen (p. 244)

Dinner
- ⅔ cup low-fat natural yogurt

WEEK 4	Day 1	Day 2

Breakfast
- La Dolce Vita (p. 243)

Dinner
- ⅔ cup low-fat natural yogurt
- 1 cup cucumber strips

Breakfast
- Smooth Moves (p. 248)

Dinner
- ⅔ cup low-fat natural yogurt

Cool Moves

3-Day Cleanse and Detox Meal Plan

	Breakfast	Lunch	Dinner
Day 1	Grapefruit and Pomegranate Zinger (p. 255)	Apple Teaser (p. 256)	½ serving Hot Saucy Mama (p. 190)
Day 2	Melonberry Joy (p. 259)	Mint and Lime Crush (p. 255)	Spicy Bean Salad (p. 312)
Day 3	Green Tea Refresher (p. 256)	Strawberry Blush (p. 263)	Brown Rice and Vegetable Salad (p. 305)

Just for Kids

7-Day Healthy Eating Plan for Growing Children

This plan provides about 1,800 calories per day, to meet the average calorie needs of a moderately active 9- or 10-year old. Quantities can be adjusted according to gender, age, and level of hunger. "Moderately active" means including physical activity equivalent to walking 1.5 to 3 miles per day at 3 to 4 miles per hour, in addition to the light physical activity associated with daily life.

Day 1

Breakfast
- Monkey Business (p. 267)
- 1 slice grainy toast with 2 tsp peanut butter

Lunch
- 3 multigrain crackers with 3 tbsp hummus
- 1 cup carrot strips
- 1 cup celery strips
- 1 cup watermelon cubes
- ⅔ cup low-fat natural yogurt

Dinner
- Tuna Patties (p. 314)
- ½ steamed corn cob with ½ tsp butter
- ½ cup steamed green beans
- ½ cup steamed snow peas
- ½ cup apple juice

Snacks
- 1 cup skim milk
- 1 tbsp reduced-fat cheese
- 5 walnut halves
- 1½ tbsp golden raisins
- 1½ cups air-popped popcorn
- 1 apple

Day 2

Breakfast
- Oats with Bananas and Maple Syrup (p. 308)
- ½ cup apple juice

Lunch
- Slimy Green Monster (p. 268)
- Grainy sandwich with 1 tsp margarine, 1 oz (2 tbsp) reduced-fat cheese, and ½ cup lettuce

Dinner
- Honey-Baked Pumpkin Risotto (p. 307)
- ½ cup raw broccoli florets
- ½ cup red bell pepper
- 1 cup peeled and de-seeded cantaloupe

Snacks
- ⅔ cup low-fat natural yogurt
- 1 pear
- 2 rice cakes with 1 tsp margarine and 2 tsp nut spread
- 1 tbsp cashews with 1½ tbsp currants

301

Day 3

Breakfast
- ¾ cup whole grain breakfast cereal with ½ cup skim milk, 1 tsp honey, and ½ cup berries
- 1 cup skim milk with 1 tbsp Ovaltine™

Lunch
- Grainy sandwich with 2 tbsp avocado, 2 oz shaved chicken breast, and ¼ cup alfalfa sprouts
- 1 apple
- 1 tbsp reduced-fat cheese

Dinner
- Crunchy Fish (p. 306)
- Nutty Sweet Potato (p. 308)
- ½ cup lettuce with ½ cup cherry tomatoes and 1 carrot

Snacks
- Orange and Mango Spider (p. 272)
- ⅔ cup low-fat natural yogurt
- 1 banana
- 2 celery stalks with 1 tbsp peanut butter
- 1 carrot
- ½ oz milk chocolate

Day 4

Breakfast
- Manana Bango (p. 275)
- 1 wheat breakfast biscuit topped with 1 tsp nut spread and 1 sliced banana

Lunch
- Grainy sandwich with 2 tsp margarine, 1 oz (2 tbsp) reduced-fat cheese, ½ grated carrot, and ½ cup lettuce leaves

Dinner
- Sweet Lemony Salmon (p. 313)
- ½ cup brown rice cooked according to package's instructions
- ½ cup steamed green beans
- ½ cup steamed asparagus
- 1 cup watermelon

Snacks
- ⅔ cup low-fat natural yogurt
- 1 fruit and nut trail mix/granola bar
- 1 cup skim milk with 1 tbsp Ovaltine™

Day 5

Breakfast
- ½ cup natural muesli with ½ cup skim milk
- ½ whole grain English muffin with 1 tsp margarine and 1 tsp honey
- 1 cup orange juice

Lunch
- 4 rice cakes with 2 tsp margarine and 1 tbsp nut spread
- 1 pear

Dinner
- Eggplant Pasta (p. 306)
- ½ cup raw broccoli florets
- 1 carrot
- 2 celery stalks

Snacks
- Tutti Frutti (p. 277)
- ⅔ cup low-fat natural yogurt
- 1 cup skim milk
- 2 multigrain rice cakes with 1 tbsp reduced-fat cheese

Margarine and Butter: If a recipe calls for margarine, choose one that is monounsaturated or polyunsaturated, and free of trans fats. For children, who follow an otherwise healthy diet and do not have heart disease, a small amount of butter may be used.

Day 6

Breakfast

- 2 slices grainy toast with 2 tsp margarine and 1 tbsp avocado, topped with 1 egg cooked in 1 tsp olive oil
- ½ cup apple juice

Lunch

- Chocaberry Blitz (p. 277)
- 3 large multigrain crackers with 3 tbsp hummus and 1 grated carrot
- 2 kiwifruits

Dinner

- Chickpea and Potato Soup (p. 305)
- 1 grainy dinner roll with 1 tsp margarine

Snacks

- ⅔ cup low-fat natural yogurt
- 2 cups celery and bell pepper strips
- 1 cup skim milk
- 3 tbsp golden raisins
- 1 tbsp reduced-fat cheese
- 1 small homemade muffin

Day 7

Breakfast

- 2 slices grainy toast with 2 tsp margarine
- 1 small can baked beans
- 1 cup watermelon
- 1 cup skim milk with 1 tbsp Ovaltine™

Lunch

- Orange Fizz (p. 274)
- Grainy sandwich with 2 tsp margarine and 1 sliced banana
- a small handful of cashews

Dinner

- Sweet Potato Frittata (p. 313)
- ½ cup lettuce with ½ cup cherry tomatoes
- 1 cup apple juice

Snacks

- ⅔ cup low-fat natural yogurt
- 1 carrot
- 1 tbsp reduced-fat cheese
- 1¾ oz fruit and nut trail mix/granola bar
- 3 plain sweet biscuits

Recipes

Balsamic Salad

1 cup baby spinach leaves
1 chopped cucumber with skin
1 cup red and yellow cherry tomatoes
1 tsp olive oil
1 tsp balsamic vinegar

Toss vegetables together and drizzle with olive oil and vinegar.

Bean Thread Noodle Salad with Poached Chicken

2½ oz bean thread noodles
3½ oz skinless chicken breast
3 stalks sliced celery
a few peppercorns
1 carrot, sliced finely lengthwise
½ cup shredded red cabbage
1 sliced spring onion
1 red de-seeded chili pepper
1 tsp reduced-sodium soy sauce
1 tsp rice wine
squeeze of fresh lime juice
1 tbsp unsalted peanuts
pinch of sugar

Cook noodles according to package instructions, and refresh under cold water. Place chicken in a pot of cold water with celery and pepper, bring to boil, remove from heat, cover, and let sit for one hour. Remove chicken from water, cool slightly, and shred with a fork. Combine noodles, chicken, and vegetables together with soy sauce, rice wine, lime juice, and a pinch of sugar. Scatter peanuts over salad and serve.

Bircher Muesli

½ cup rolled oats
⅔ cup low-fat natural yogurt

Combine ingredients, cover, and refrigerate overnight. Serve chilled.

Variations:
—**with Berries:** Add 1½ tbsp golden raisins to oats before refrigerating. Top with 1 cup of mixed berries just before serving.
—**with Apple:** Stir in 1 grated apple and 1½ tbsp of currants just before serving.
—**with Apple, Cinnamon, and Almonds:** Stir in 1 grated apple, ¼ tsp cinnamon, and 10 roughly chopped almonds just before serving.

Note for Vegetarians:

A portion of meat is equal to any of the following:

- 4 oysters
- 3 king prawns
- 1⅔ oz raw skinless chicken breast
- 1½ oz canned tuna (drained)
- 1⅔ oz raw white fleshed fish
- 2 oz raw salmon

and may be exchanged with any of these:

- ⅓ cup legumes
- 2⅔ oz tofu
- 1 small egg
- ⅔ oz low-fat cheese

Brown Rice with Tuna and Kidney Beans

½ cup brown rice
⅓ cup kidney beans (rinsed and drained)
3 oz tuna (in springwater, drained)
1 cup baby spinach leaves
a handful of fresh parsley
freshly cracked black pepper
squeeze of lemon juice

Cook the rice according to the instructions on the package. Cool, then combine with the other ingredients.

Brown Rice and Vegetable Salad

2 tbsp brown rice
½ clove garlic, sliced
¼ red onion, sliced
½ red bell pepper, sliced
½ raw zucchini, grated
1 grated raw beet
a handful of fresh parsley
squeeze of fresh lemon juice
1 tsp freshly grated lemon zest

Cook the rice according to package instructions, then cool. Separately, cook the garlic, red onion, and bell pepper in a small nonstick frying pan until soft, adding a little water if necessary. Allow to cool. Combine the rice and vegetables with the zucchini, beet, parsley, lemon juice, and zest, then serve.

Chickpea and Potato Soup

¼ onion, finely sliced
¼ red bell pepper, finely sliced
2 tsp olive oil
¼ tsp cumin
¼ tsp ground coriander
¼ tsp cinnamon
1 cup reduced-sodium stock
1 cubed potato
⅓ cup canned chickpeas (rinsed and drained)

Cook the onion and bell pepper in a saucepan with the olive oil until soft. Add the remaining ingredients and cook for 20–25 minutes until potato is soft.

Chili Swiss Chard

1 tsp olive oil
2 cups sliced Swiss chard
½ clove garlic, sliced
1 de-seeded red chili pepper

Heat the olive oil in a nonstick frying pan. Add the Swiss chard, garlic, and chili pepper and stir until chard has wilted.

Chili Tomato Spaghetti

3½ oz spaghetti
½ red onion, finely sliced
1 tsp olive oil
2 cups red and yellow cherry tomatoes
1 finely sliced garlic clove
1 sliced de-seeded chili pepper
a handful of fresh basil
¾ oz shaved Parmesan

Cook the spaghetti until al dente. In a nonstick frying pan, cook the onion in the olive oil until lightly brown. Add the tomatoes and cook for a few minutes until they are just collapsing. Stir through the garlic and chili pepper, then mix in the spaghetti and basil. Top with the Parmesan cheese.

Crisp Vegetable and Tofu Stir-Fry

⅓ cup brown rice
8 sliced asparagus spears
1 cup broccoli florets
1 cup sliced red bell pepper
1 cup sliced bok choy
a handful of roughly chopped cilantro
1 sliced garlic clove
1 sliced red chili pepper
2 tsp reduced-sodium soy sauce
2 tsp sesame oil
1 tbsp vegetable stock
2¾ oz silken tofu

Cook brown rice according to package instructions and keep warm. Mix all the remaining ingredients except the stock and the tofu together in a mixing bowl. Heat the vegetable stock in a wok, add the vegetables, and cook for 3–4 minutes. Add the tofu to warm through, and serve with the brown rice.

Crunchy Fish

3½ oz flathead tails
1 beaten egg
2 tbsp rice flour
1 tbsp quinoa flakes
1 tsp olive oil

Dip the flathead tails in a little of the beaten egg, then coat with rice flour. Dip the coated tails into the remaining egg, then coat with the quinoa flakes. Cook in the olive oil in a nonstick frying pan for 1–2 minutes on each side.

Eggplant Pasta

2¾ oz spaghetti
¼ red onion, finely sliced
2 tsp olive oil
½ garlic clove, crushed
1 finely chopped basil stem
and 8–10 leaves
¼ eggplant, cubed
3½ oz canned tomatoes with juice

Cook spaghetti until al dente. In a nonstick frying pan, cook the onion in the olive oil until lightly browned. Add the garlic, basil stem, and eggplant. When eggplant is soft, add the tomatoes and simmer for 15 minutes. Stir basil leaves into the pasta, combine with the eggplant mixture, and serve.

Farro and Lentil Salad

⅓ cup farro
1 cup cubed pumpkin
⅔ cup canned brown lentils (rinsed and drained)
1 cup baby spinach leaves
1 finely sliced spring onion
1½ tbsp currants
1 tsp pine nuts
a handful of fresh parsley
1 tsp olive oil
squeeze of fresh lemon juice

Mix ingredients together in a bowl and serve.

Fettucini with Sweet Onion and Kale

3½ oz fettucini

2 cups kale leaves, with woody stems removed

½ red onion, finely sliced

2 tsp olive oil

1 chopped garlic clove

½ tsp grated lemon zest

1½ oz (3 tbsp) shaved Parmesan cheese

Cook the fettucini until al dente. Finely slice the kale and place in a large pot of boiling water for 2–3 minutes. Refresh under cold running water. Meanwhile, cook onion with olive oil in a nonstick frying pan over low heat until brown and sticky. Add garlic and cook for another minute. Add kale, stir to warm through and coat it in the onion mixture. Remove from heat, then add the lemon zest and cheese. Stir in the fettucini, then serve.

Garden Salad

2 cups baby spinach

1 cucumber, sliced

1 cup cherry tomatoes

1 sliced carrot

a handful of fresh parsley

squeeze of lemon juice

1 tsp olive oil

Combine all ingredients then serve.

Green Salad

2 cups watercress

1 sliced cucumber

¼ cup alfalfa

2 tbsp avocado

1 tsp olive oil

squeeze of fresh lemon juice

Combine all ingredients then serve.

Honey-Baked Pumpkin Risotto

¼ cup cubed pumpkin

2 tsp olive oil

1 tsp honey

¼ onion, finely chopped

¼ leek, finely chopped

1 celery stalk, finely chopped

¼ carrot, finely chopped

2½ oz arborio rice

1 cup reduced-sodium vegetable stock

½ tbsp Parmesan cheese

Place the pumpkin in a baking tray with half the oil and cook at 350° F for 15 minutes. Stir in the honey and cook for a further 10–15 minutes. Meanwhile, heat remaining olive oil in a lidded saucepan, then sauté the onion, leek, celery, and carrot until soft. Add the rice, stir for a minute, then add the stock. Cover with lid and simmer for about 18 minutes. Remove from heat and stir in the Parmesan and pumpkin. Allow to sit for a few minutes before serving.

Moroccan Chickpea and Quinoa Chicken Salad

5 oz skinless chicken breast
3 stalks sliced celery
a few peppercorns
⅓ cup quinoa
⅓ cup canned chickpeas (rinsed and drained)
2 sliced spring onions
½ pomegranate (seeds only)
1 tsp cumin
1 tsp olive oil

Place the chicken in a pot of cold water with celery and peppercorns and bring to boil. Turn off heat, cover, and allow to sit for one hour. Remove from water, cool slightly, then shred with a fork. Meanwhile, prepare the quinoa according to the package instructions. Combine chicken, quinoa, chickpeas, spring onions, pomegranate seeds, cumin, and olive oil. Toss well and serve.

Nutty Sweet Potato

5 oz sweet potato with skin
1 tsp maple syrup
1 tsp margarine
1 tbsp roughly chopped walnuts

Steam the sweet potato, until just soft. Cut a cross in the top and mash the maple syrup, margarine, and walnuts into the flesh with a fork. Serve.

Variations:
—**"Just for Kids"**: For this meal plan, reduce to 3½ oz sweet potato.
—**Potato and Parsnip Mash:** Omit maple syrup and walnuts and replace sweet potatoes with 5oz peeled potatoes and ½ of a parsnip. Steam as above, then mash together with margarine and 1 tsp of olive oil. Whip until smooth.

Oats with Bananas and Maple Syrup

½ cup rolled oats
½ cup skim milk
1½ tbsp golden raisins
2 tsp maple syrup
½ banana, peeled and sliced

Cook the oats with the skim milk, adding a little extra water if needed. Remove from heat, stir in the raisins and maple syrup, and top with sliced bananas.

Poached Chicken with Italian Tomatoes

5 oz skinless chicken breast
1 stalk sliced celery
a few peppercorns
1 cup cherry tomatoes, halved
½ garlic clove, crushed
1 tbsp finely sliced basil leaves
1 tsp olive oil

Place chicken, celery, and pepper in a pot of cold water and bring to boil. Remove from heat, cover, and let sit for 1 hour. Combine tomatoes, garlic, basil, and olive oil and allow to sit at room temperature. Remove chicken from saucepan and top with tomato mix.

Poached Chicken with Quinoa, Almonds, and Pear

5 oz skinless chicken breast

2 stalks celery

a few peppercorns

⅓ cup quinoa

10 chopped almonds

1 cup sliced cherry tomatoes

1 tbsp chopped parsley

⅓ cup canned cannellini beans, (rinsed and drained)

1 de-seeded and finely sliced pear

1 finely sliced spring onion

1 cup baby spinach leaves

1 tsp olive oil

1 tsp white wine vinegar

1 tsp whole-grain mustard

Place chicken in a pot of cold water with celery and pepper, bring to boil, remove from heat, cover, and let sit for one hour. Remove chicken from water, cool slightly, and shred with a fork. Meanwhile, prepare the quinoa according to the package instructions, then allow to cool. Combine the quinoa with the almonds, tomatoes, parsley, cannellini beans, pear, spring onion, spinach leaves, and shredded chicken. To dress, mix together the olive oil, vinegar, and mustard, then drizzle over the top.

Poached Mackerel

5 oz mackerel

2 stalks sliced celery

a few peppercorns

a handful of parsley

Simmer mackerel for 7 minutes in a covered saucepan with half an inch of boiling water together with celery, peppercorns, and parsley.

Variations:

—**Poached Mackerel with Mango Salsa:** Make salsa by mixing together ½ of a peeled, pitted, and cubed mango, 1 finely sliced spring onion, 1 tbsp cilantro leaves, and a squeeze of lime juice. Simmer mackerel as above, omitting the celery, then serve with mango salsa.

—**Poached Salmon:** Replace mackerel with 5 oz of salmon.

—**Poached Salmon and Ginger:** Simmer 3½ oz salmon in water for 7 minutes. Remove from saucepan and top with ½ tsp of grated ginger and 1 finely sliced spring onion. Pour 1 tsp of warmed olive oil over the top and serve. (Omit celery, peppercorns, and parsley.)

Prawn Stir-Fry with Wild Rice

⅓ cup brown rice

½ finely sliced onion

2 sliced celery stalks

1 cup broccoli florets

½ sliced red bell pepper

1 cup sliced bok choy

1 handful fresh cilantro

1 sliced red chili pepper (de-seeded if desired)

1 tsp reduced-sodium soy sauce

1 tsp sesame oil

6 peeled and de-veined prawns

10 cashew nuts

Cook the rice according to the package instructions. Meanwhile, toss the onion, celery, broccoli, bell pepper, bok choy, cilantro, and chili pepper together in a bowl. Drizzle with soy sauce. In a wok, heat the sesame oil, add the prawns, and cook for two minutes on each side. Add the vegetable mixture and stir-fry for 2–3 minutes. Top with the cashew nuts and serve with rice.

Pumpkin, Chickpea, and Beet Couscous

⅓ cup couscous
½ tsp Moroccan spice blend
1 cup peeled, de-seeded, and cubed pumpkin
1 tsp olive oil
⅓ cup canned chickpeas (rinsed and drained)
1 cup baby spinach leaves
4–5 canned baby beets, drained
a handful of fresh mint

Add the spice blend to the couscous and prepare in water according to the package instructions. Meanwhile, bake the pumpkin with the olive oil for 30 minutes at 350° F. Allow pumpkin and couscous to cool, mix together with the chickpeas, spinach, beets, and mint, then serve cold or at room temperature.

Rattatouille

⅓ cup brown rice
¼ cup chopped onion
1 tbsp olive oil
1 tsp cumin
1 tsp ground coriander
½ red bell pepper, cut into 1-in squares
½ green bell pepper, cut into 1-in squares
½ eggplant, cubbed
1 roughly chopped zucchini
1 cup peeled, de-seeded, and cubed pumpkin
7 oz canned tomatoes and juice
a large handful of fresh parsley
10 pitted green olives

Cook the rice according to the package instructions. Meanwhile, in a large saucepan, cook the onion in the olive oil for 4–5 minutes. Add the spices and stir for another minute. Add the bell peppers, eggplant, zucchini, and pumpkin. Stir over medium heat until the vegetables are coated in the onion and spices. Add the tomatoes and simmer for 35–40 minutes. Stir in the parsley and olives, remove from heat, and serve with rice.

Raw Beet and Chickpea Salad

⅓ cup couscous
½ tsp pumpkin pie spice
1½ cup cubed pumpkin
1 raw grated beet
1 cup baby spinach leaves
1 tsp olive oil
4 chopped mint leaves
¼ cup currants

Prepare the couscous according to the package instructions, then stir in the spice. Steam the pumpkin cubes. Allow to cool, then add the beet, spinach, olive oil, mint leaves, currants, and couscous, then serve.

Red Bell Pepper and Spinach Omelet

¼ red onion, sliced
½ red bell pepper, sliced
1 tsp olive oil
1 cup baby spinach
2 lightly beaten eggs

In a small frying pan, sauté the onion and bell pepper in half the olive oil until soft. Stir through spinach until just wilted. Remove vegetables and wipe pan clean. Heat the remaining oil in pan, then add the eggs. When almost set, place the mixture on one half, fold the other half over the top, cook for a further minute or so, then serve.

Smoked Salmon and Dill Frittata

5 oz potatoes, sliced
1 tsp olive oil
2 beaten eggs
1 chopped slice of smoked salmon
a small handful of roughly chopped dill

Steam the potatoes until tender. Heat the olive oil in a small oven-proof frying pan, then add the eggs. When the eggs are just beginning to set underneath, layer the potato, salmon, and dill into the egg and continue to cook until egg is browning underneath. Set the top under a broiler before serving.

Snow Pea Salad

1 cup watercress
½ cup raw snow peas
½ cup cherry tomatoes
2 tbsp alfalfa sprouts
squeeze of fresh lemon juice

Mix ingredients together in a bowl and serve.

Soba Noodles with Marinated Salmon and Greens

3½ oz fresh skinless salmon
1 tsp fresh grated ginger
½ garlic clove, crushed
1 tsp reduced-sodium soy sauce
1 tsp mirin (sweet rice wine)
2 tsp sesame oil
⅓ cup soba noodles
1 cup bok choy
1 cup broccolini
1 cup green beans
1 tbsp toasted
sesame seeds

Place salmon in a bowl with ginger, garlic, soy sauce, mirin, and half the sesame oil and marinate for 20–30 minutes. Meanwhile, prepare soba noodles according to package instructions. Cook salmon with the remaining sesame oil in a nonstick frying pan for 3–4 minutes on each side. Separately, steam the bok choy, broccolini, and green beans. Top noodles with salmon and vegetables, and sprinkle with the sesame seeds.

Spaghetti with Prawns and Spinach

3½ oz spaghetti or linguini
2 tsp olive oil
½ clove garlic, sliced
1 red de-seeded chili pepper
6 shelled and de-veined king prawns
1 cup baby spinach leaves

Cook pasta until al dente. Heat olive oil in a nonstick frying pan, and add the garlic, chili pepper, and prawns. Cook for 3–4 minutes. Stir in the pasta and spinach leaves.

Spiced Chickpea Couscous

⅓ cup couscous

1 tsp cumin

½ pomegranate (seeds only)

1 tbsp chopped parsley

1 small grated zucchini

1 tsp olive oil

squeeze of fresh lemon juice

Add the cumin to the couscous then cook the couscous according to the package instructions. Cool slightly, combine with pomegranate seeds, parsley, zucchini, olive oil, and lemon juice, then serve.

Spiced Chickpeas and Pumpkin

2 cups peeled and de-seeded pumpkin

1 tsp olive oil

½ tsp cumin

⅔ cup canned chickpeas (rinsed and drained)

1 tbsp pine nuts

1 cup baby spinach leaves

Mix together the pumpkin, olive oil, and cumin, and bake at 350° F for 30 minutes. Remove from oven and stir through the chickpeas, pine nuts, and spinach. Serve warm.

Spiced Farro and Eggplant Salad

½ cup farro

¼ onion, finely sliced

½ garlic clove, sliced

2 tsp olive oil

¼ tsp each of turmeric, cinnamon, and pumpkin pie spice

⅓ cup canned brown lentils (rinsed and drained)

1 apple, cored, de-seeded, and diced

1½ tbsp currants

1 eggplant

a handful of roughly chopped mint

a handful of roughly chopped cilantro

2 tbsp low-fat natural yogurt

Cook farro according to package instructions. Meanwhile, cook the onion, garlic, and spices in 1 teaspoon of the olive oil. Remove from heat and stir in the cooked farro and lentils. Cool slightly, then stir through the apple and currants and allow to cool completely. Meanwhile, cut eggplant into wedges, brush with remaining olive oil, and roast at 350° F for 20 minutes or until soft. Serve farro mixture topped with eggplant, mint, cilantro, and yogurt.

Spicy Bean Salad

½ tomato, chopped

½ fresh corn cob, kernels only

⅔ cup canned chickpeas (rinsed and drained)

1 sliced spring onion

1 chopped cucumber

½ red bell pepper, chopped

1 cup sliced baby spinach leaves

2 tsp balsamic vinegar

tiny pinch of chili powder

Combine all ingredients except vinegar and chili powder. Separately, mix the vinegar and chili powder together to make a dressing, then toss over the vegetables to serve.

Stir-Fried Tofu and Greens

⅓ cup brown rice
2 tsp sesame oil
1 cup bok choy
1 cup broccolini
1 cup green beans
½ clove garlic, sliced
1 de-seeded and sliced red chili pepper
a handful of fresh cilantro
3½ oz sliced silken tofu

Cook brown rice according to package instructions. Meanwhile, heat the sesame oil in a wok. Add the bok choy, broccolini, and green beans, and stir-fry for 1–2 minutes. Add the garlic, chili pepper, cilantro, and silken tofu. Toss gently until tofu is warm, then serve with rice.

Sweet and Tasty Brown Rice Salad

½ cup brown rice
1 cup cubed sweet potato
1½ tbsp currants
1 cup watercress, roughly chopped
a handful of sliced fresh mint
1 tbsp orange juice
1 tsp olive oil

Cook brown rice according to instructions on the package. Steam the sweet potato. When both have cooled, combine with the other ingredients and mix well.

Sweet Lemony Salmon

2 tsp olive oil
½ tsp lemon zest
2 tsp honey
3½ oz salmon fillet

Heat the olive oil with the lemon zest and honey in a nonstick frying pan. Add the salmon fillet and cook for 3–4 minutes on each side. Serve with half a cup each of cooked brown rice, steamed green beans, and steamed asparagus.

Sweet Potato Frittata

2 oz sliced sweet potato
½ sliced onion
¼ sliced red bell pepper
1 tsp olive oil
1 cup baby spinach leaves
2 lightly whisked eggs
½ tbsp grated Parmesan

Cook sweet potato over low heat in an oven-proof pan with onion, bell pepper, and half the olive oil, then stir through spinach. Remove vegetables, wipe pan clean, then add remaining olive oil and eggs. When just beginning to set, add the vegetables, sprinkle Parmesan over the top, then finish the frittata under the broiler.

Tuna Nicoise Salad

5 oz boiled and sliced fingerling potatoes

1 poached egg

8–10 steamed green beans

3 oz canned tuna (in springwater, drained)

⅓ cup kidney beans

10 pitted olives

2 cups romaine lettuce leaves

a handful of fresh parsley

1 tsp whole-grain mustard

1 tsp olive oil

1 tsp white wine vinegar

1½ tbsp shaved Parmesan cheese

Combine the potatoes, egg, green beans, tuna, kidney beans, olives, lettuce, and parsley in a salad bowl. Separately, mix together the mustard, olive oil, and vinegar to make the dressing. Toss the dressing through the salad, top with Parmesan cheese, then serve.

Tuna Patties

1½ potatoes

1½ oz canned tuna (in springwater, drained)

a handful of parsley

2 tbsp rice flour

1 tbsp olive oil

Steam potatoes until tender. Mash together with tuna and parsley. Form into 2–3 small patties, coat with rice flour, then cook gently with the olive oil in a nonstick frying pan, turning occasionally, until brown on both sides.

Vegetable Frittata

4 oz sliced sweet potato

½ onion, sliced

¼ red bell pepper, sliced

1 tsp olive oil

1 cup baby spinach leaves

2 lightly whisked eggs

Cook sweet potato with onion, bell pepper, and half the olive oil over low heat in an oven-proof pan, then stir in the spinach. Remove vegetables, wipe pan clean, then add remaining olive oil and eggs. When just beginning to set, add the vegetables, then finish the frittata under the broiler.

Vietnamese Rice Noodle Salad

2 oz rice noodles

1 cup bean sprouts

½ cup shredded red cabbage

1 julienned carrot

2 finely sliced radishes

a handful of fresh mint leaves

1 finely sliced red chili (de-seeded if desired)

2 tsp sesame seeds

1 tsp rice wine

squeeze of fresh lime juice

pinch of sugar

Cook the noodles according to package instructions, then refresh under cold water. Combine with all ingredients except the rice wine, lime juice, and sugar. Separately, combine these three ingredients together to make a dressing, then toss through the noodles and vegetables.

Watercress Salad with Chicken, Pear, and Walnuts

3½ oz skinless chicken breast

2 stalks sliced celery

a few peppercorns

½ cup brown rice

2 cups watercress

1 cored, de-seeded, and sliced pear

1 small sliced cucumber

1 tbsp chopped walnuts

1 tsp olive oil (or walnut oil)

1 tsp white wine vinegar

1 finely sliced spring onion

Place chicken in a pot of cold water with celery and pepper, and bring to boil. Remove from heat, cover, and let sit for one hour. Remove chicken from water, cool slightly, and shred with a fork. Meanwhile, prepare the rice according to package instructions. When chicken and rice are cool, combine with the watercress, pear, cucumber, and walnuts. Toss through the olive oil, vinegar, and spring onion and serve.

Wild Rice Salad with Chickpeas and Mango

½ cup wild rice

⅓ cup canned brown lentils (rinsed and drained)

⅔ cup canned chickpeas (rinsed and drained)

1 tbsp pine nuts

1 cup cherry tomatoes

½ mango, sliced

a handful of fresh parsley leaves

1 tsp olive oil

squeeze of fresh lime juice

Prepare the rice according to the package instructions. Cool, then add the lentils, chickpeas, pine nuts, tomatoes, mangoes, and parsley. Separately, combine the olive oil and lime juice, then drizzle over the salad to serve.

Zucchini Basil Pasta

2⅔ oz pasta

1 grated zucchini

a handful of fresh chopped basil

1 cup halved cherry tomatoes

2 tsp olive oil

½ tsp finely grated lemon zest

Cook the pasta until al dente, then drain. Return pasta to the saucepan and stir through the zucchini, basil, tomatoes, olive oil, and zest, then serve.

Zucchini Linguini

3½ oz linguini

1 grated zucchini

a handful of fresh parsley

1 cup baby spinach leaves

1 tsp freshly grated lemon zest

squeeze of fresh lemon juice

2 tsp olive oil

Cook the linguini until al dente, drain, then return to pan. Stir through the other ingredients and serve.

Index

Photo Credits

Multiple credits per page are listed in a clockwise sequence.